THE DEATH OF CAPTAIN COOK

The Death of
CAPTAIN COOK

Gavin Kennedy

Duckworth

First published in 1978 by
Gerald Duckworth & Co. Ltd
The Old Piano Factory
43 Gloucester Crescent, London NW1

ISBN 0 7156 0956 4

Photoset by
Specialised Offset Services Ltd., Liverpool
Printed in Great Britain by The Anchor Press Ltd.
and bound by Wm Brendon & Son Ltd.
both of Tiptree, Essex

Contents

List of Illustrations   vii

Preface   1

1. Captain Cook and his Officers   7

2. The Return of Lono   17

3. Edgar's Folly   28

4. Theft of the Cutter   37

5. A Change of Plan   45

6. Cook Thwarted   56

7. The Death of Captain Cook   67

8. The Aftermath   81

Bibliography   95

Index   101

FOR JEAN

Illustrations

(between pages 48 and 49)

1. The title page of the official account of Captain Cook's last voyage, written by Cook and, after his death, James King, and published in 1784.
2. The Cook Memorial Medal struck by the Royal Society to commemorate him after his death.
3. Portrait of Captain James King from the title page of Vol. III of the official account.
4. 'Terreeoboo, King of Owyhee, bringing presents to Captain Cook', from Cook and King, 1784.
5. 'A view of Karakakooa in Owyhee', from Cook and King, 1784.
6. Bligh's chart of Kealakekua Bay, from Cook and King, 1784.
7. A portable observatory of the type used on Cook's last voyage.
8. 'An offering before Captain Cook, in the Sandwich Islands', from Cook and King, 1784.
9. 'A morai in Atooi', from Cook and King, 1784.
10. The death of Cook, by John Webber.
11. The death of Cook, engraving by Hall after a painting by George Carter.
12. The death of Cook, by Johann Zoffany.
13. The death of Cook, a coloured aquatint by F. Jukes after a picture by John Clevely, based on a drawing by James Clevely, his brother, who was a carpenter on the *Resolution*.

Preface

Captain Cook was killed by Hawaiians on the morning of Sunday 14 February 1779 at Kealakekua Bay, Hawaii. In the two centuries since 1779, much has been written about his career, his achievements and his death; it is remarkable that in all the literature there has been no definitive account of what happened at Kealakekua.

Within Cook's own entourage, various views about the cause of his death emerged in the years that followed. Some were precursors of the missionary version, such as John Ledyard's famous and popular account that treated Cook's death as retribution for his acceptance of godhood from the Hawaiians (Munford, 1963a). Others blamed his over-confidence in dealing with the islanders. The various ms. journal accounts, based on reports from the only eye-witness, tended to this view. Lieutenant King's official version, in the published account of Cook's three voyages (King, 1784), allowed that Cook might have been hasty, though he also tried to lay the blame indirectly on Lieutenant Rickman. These journals and King's book provoked counter-accounts, such as that of the Assistant Surgeon, Samwell (1786), which went to great lengths to show that Captain Cook was careful and cautious in everything he did, even to the extent of saying that it was not Cook's crews who introduced venereal disease to the islands.

When Kippis published his narrative of Cook's voyage in 1788, mostly following Samwell's interpretation, he established himself as an informed and authoritative biographer, whose discussion of Cook's life stands up well to modern criticism. He introduced to a wider audience the journals of several of Cook's compatriots on the voyage, and opened up to public discussion the questionable actions of Lieutenant Williamson, which had been glossed over in King's official version. Kippis' book remained in print for sixty years, but never gained the authority of King's version, which was repeated in dozens of popular books and many learned ones as well, although, as I shall show, it is in parts highly contentious.

William Bligh, later commander of H.M.S. *Bounty*, was the Master of the *Resolution* on this voyage of Cook's. He had been appointed to this important post at the astonishingly young age of twenty-four. Bligh has been accused (Hough, 1972) of causing the death of Captain Cook, though indirectly and unintentionally. Bligh fired at a Hawaiian canoe on the morning of the 14th, and Lieutenant Rickman, allegedly emulating Bligh, fired at another canoe and killed a local chief. One argument is that the news of Rickman's action, once announced to the crowd of Hawaiians around Captain Cook's party, inflamed their anger and sealed Cook's fate. Lieutenant King's official account of the voyage failed to give William Bligh any credit for his undoubted contribution to its achievements, and went so far as to plagiarise his charts and drawings and credit them to Lieutenant Roberts. Those who blame Bligh for Cook's death take this as evidence that the other officers disapproved of Bligh's behaviour and took this informal action in retribution for his part in Cook's death.

Thus the death of Captain Cook has been credited to several different causes. Whether Cook was careless, or whether Bligh, Rickman or anyone else was responsible, could, one would imagine, be tested by appealing to the journals and published reports of the persons present on that morning. But this is made difficult by the absence of eye-witness accounts. While there are several reports and journals available by officers who were present in the bay, the only officer who actually landed with Cook was Lieutenant of Marines Molesworth Phillips. We have not got his own written account of what happened, which was apparently extant until at least 1849, but was then lost (Beaglehole, 1955-69, p.clxxvi). However, he did report what he saw in detail to the officers on the ships, and they in turn wrote down what he told them and incorporated his remarks in their journals. Even so, there were numerous contradictions in the several versions that emerged from these report sessions. (To give a small example: King's official version (1784) states that Phillips was severely wounded in the shoulder; but Edgar and Law, Master and Surgeon on the *Discovery*, in their ms. accounts state merely that he 'received a slight wound'.)

Munford (1963b) discusses the theory that John Ledyard, the marine corporal whose account of Cook's death was published two years later, was with Cook in the shore party; but it seems most likely that he was actually with the other shore party across the bay. Lieutenant Henry Roberts, in command of the Captain's pinnace just off the shore, is the nearest eye-witness to have left a written report (Roberts, ms. Log). Naturally, his account exculpates himself. Lieutenant Williamson, in command of the other boat further along the shore, does not seem to have left an account, which is a pity. His earlier Journal, fragments of which survive (Williamson, ms. Log and Proceedings) shows that he was a perceptive observer and open critic of those around him. Martin, Mate of the launch, and Lanyon, midshipman, wrote accounts (Martin, 1779; Lanyon, 1779) and were close by the action. All the other accounts of the incident are composite versions drawn from interviews with those who were present or inferences from the gossip that swept the ships. Reconciling the reports is an exceptionally difficult task.

In the following chapters, I have brought together the known versions of the incidents that led to Cook's hasty venture ashore on 14 February 1779, and of subsequent events, and examined them for a coherent and probable explanation of what happened. The story is told in chronological order, from the theft of the armourer's tongs on the *Discovery* about 4.00 p.m. on 13 February to the retreat from the bay at noon on 14 February, and variations in the accounts are discussed as it unfolds. Inevitably there are some time-consuming diversions, but I hope that this method makes comparison of the contradictions clearer by presenting them in context.

A viewpoint often ignored is that of the Hawaiians themselves. As they had no written language until the missionaries arrived, their version of the story of Captain Cook and his visits to the islands remained for some time a purely oral tradition. In this form it rapidly degenerated into a barely recognisable tale coloured by myth and fantasy (Stokes, 1930; Coffin, 1875; Searle, 1920). When the missionaries descended on the Pacific islands in the nineteenth century they had their own axe to grind; they managed to turn Cook's death from an accident of human folly into a divine intervention by God who, angered by Cook's compliance with the Hawaiian belief that he was the god Lono, struck him down in retribution for his wicked blasphemy. They persuaded generations of Hawaiians of this belief, and Cook's name became synonymous with wickedness in the islands for over a hundred years (Stokes, 1930; Bingham, 1855). As a result the Hawaiian view can only be guessed at from a consideration of their known religious and cultural beliefs, and from secondary evidence such as that of the Rev. William Ellis (1825, 1974), a missionary who wrote a great deal about local customs and also about the Hawaiian versions of Cook's death. Little notice has been taken of the Hawaiian point of view in almost all the accounts, so some useful evidence may have been ignored. I have tried to rectify that omission here.

Place names and personal names in Hawaiian can show an alarming inconsistency (see Ellis, 1974, pp. 49-54, 459-71). This is complicated by the changes that have taken place in the language since the eighteenth century. Cook's men wrote down the Hawaiian language as best they could. It was similar to the Tahitian language, which some of them had mastered on their visits to Tahiti on previous voyages; nevertheless, their acquaintance with Hawaiian was extremely limited. So the confusion over place and proper names is hardly surprising. For example, the modern Kealakekua Bay was written as Karakakooa Bay by Cook's men. The warrior chief of Hawaii, universally designated a King by the seamen and historians, was known as Terreeoboo (with numerous spellings) by Cook's men; his name is spelled Kalei'opu'u by Beaglehole (1974), with several similar variants in use in other Cook biographies. I have chosen not to modernise the spellings in a systematic way. In the main, with a few exceptions such as the modern spelling of Kealakekua Bay, I have retained the most common spellings appearing in the journals I quote from; for instance, the two villages in Kealakekua Bay are left as Bligh wrote them, Kowrowa and Kakooa. It should always be clear from the context who is being referred to and where the events are taking place.

Much of the labour of research for this book was carried out in pursuit of my biography of William Bligh (Kennedy, 1978), and therefore many of the persons who helped in that project deserve thanks for their help with this one. There were, however, a number of additional contributors who were of assistance specifically with this book. The librarian and staff of the Bernice P. Bishop Museum, Honolulu, Hawaii, in particular Cynthia Timberlake, were extremely generous with their time and resources. Professor Donald Johnson in the History Department of Hawaii University was most kind and helpful. Several Hawaiians assisted me without fuss during my stay in

Honolulu and during my visit to the 'Big Island' and Kealakekua Bay. To all these people I extend sincere thanks.

Lord Vaizey encouraged me, as ever, to undertake this project, as did Professor Alan Tait. I am once again in their debt.

The librarian and staff of the National Library of Scotland, the British Library, the Public Record Office, the Mitchell Library of New South Wales and the University of Edinburgh responded with their usual high standards of service to my many requests for assistance. Because so much of this book depends on the writings of the men who were with the *Resolution* and the *Discovery* in 1779, posthumous thanks are due to them from all scholars for their attention to the curiosity of posterity. Second only to this is the gratitude owed to the persons and institutions who preserved and protected the journals, logs and letters of the seamen and marines on Cook's last expedition, and made them available today.

For providing photographs and giving permission to reproduce them, grateful acknowledgment is made to the British Library (for 1, 4, 5, 6, 8 and 9) and the National Maritime Museum, Greenwich (for 2, 3, 7, 11, 12 and 13).

Emma Fisher of Duckworth provided her normal, but extraordinary, editorial services throughout several textual changes and re-drafts and no author could be better supported than I was by her expertise and efficiency.

Lastly, thanks are due to Patricia and Florence for making it possible for me to take the necessary time to complete this book. Without family support the labour of authorship would be heavy indeed.

Edinburgh, 1977   Gavin Kennedy

I

Captain Cook and his Officers

There are several excellent and accurate biographies of Captain James Cook available to which the reader is directed both for details of his life and for the reasons behind the Third Voyage to the Pacific in search of a northern passage to Europe. Outstanding among these are Beaglehole (1974), Kippis (1788) and Gould (1935). My purpose in this chapter is to discuss, briefly, what kind of man Cook was by the time his ships discovered Hawaii on 18 January, 1778, and what kind of men he had with him.

Cook was forty-nine years old when he first sighted the islands of Hawaii. He had achieved international prominence and acclaim late in life. He had worked his way to the rank of Post Captain in the Royal Navy by diligent effort. There was a single-mindedness about him that in retrospect seems almost calculating. He started his working life as a shop assistant, and had he survived Hawaii he might very well have ended as an Admiral. What happened in between has delighted biographers for two centuries.

We know he was exceptionally gifted as a navigator, seaman and cartographer. He had diligently acquired these skills through a long apprenticeship, first in the merchant navy on coal transports in the North Sea, and then in the Royal Navy in the cold and misty waters off Canada. He did not serve as a midshipman in the Royal Navy, in 'the cock-pit of a man of war, among young gentlemen, which is to the navy what a public school is to those who move in civil society' (quoted in Smith, 1936, p.208). He came into the Royal Navy at the late age of twenty-seven, first as an Able Bodied Seaman, and then, six months later, as Master's Mate. His experience of the merchant service as a Ship's Master made him too valuable to heave on a rope. His knowledge of the difficult arts of accurate navigation gave him his main opening for attention from his superiors, who had the power to promote, and his chance to prove what he could do if given a command and a mission. He proved himself in the relatively humble but militarily crucial task of sounding and charting the St Lawrence River for the assault on the French in Quebec during the Seven Years' War.

One success and proof of reliability led to others. By the time the war was over he was already credited with a reputation as a surveyor. Not long after, George III was persuaded by the scientific community to send an expedition to observe the transit of Venus across the sun, from the South Pacific, as part of the effort to discover the distance of the earth from the sun. Cook, who had gained through his work such sponsors as Sir Hugh Palliser, Lord Colville and Thomas Graves, Governor of Newfoundland, was chosen to command the expedition. This was his First Voyage (1768-71), and it was followed by his Second Voyage (1772-75) to search for the fabled land of *terra Australis*. In his voyages round the world Cook made the first accurate charts – in some cases the first charts – of huge areas in both southern and northern hemispheres, disproved the existence of a southern continent between Australia and South America, and pushed south into the Antarctic Circle further than anyone had been before.

It is commonplace among biographers of persons as famous as Cook to ascribe all manner of qualities to them, such as 'genius', 'charisma', 'leadership' and so on. Such faults as are known to exist are rationalised away as aberrations or interludes between superlatives. This makes it more difficult to take an unbiased look at the last hours of Cook's life. Cook's contribution to the history of the Pacific, to scientific navigation, to the health of seamen, to natural science and to geography would still have been colossal on the strength of the first two voyages alone. If instead of accepting the command of the Third Voyage he had let Lieutenant Clerke take the *Resolution* back to the Pacific, and had remained in England as a Captain of Greenwich Hospital, his greatness would not have been any the less. Therefore we must not let our respect for his achievements deter us from examining his character a little more closely and his actions a little more critically than his biographers often do.

Cook was a product of his past. He was supremely self-confident. He knew he was the best navigator and cartographer in the navy, and he knew he had the complete confidence of King George III and the

Admiralty. The discovery of Hawaii was a natural product of this confidence and of his exploratory curiosity. The way that he dawdled in the Southern Pacific, charting dozens of islands such as the Tonga group, visiting his friends on Tahiti and recording everything he could of the societies he found, shows his exploratory style in the best light. He tried not to miss anything, with the same persistence that had made his reputation in sounding the Traverse in Canada or charting the coasts of Newfoundland. Persistence distinguishes an explorer from a voyager. Cook was a dedicated explorer; he passed something of this quality to the young William Bligh.

On this voyage he had William Bligh with him as his Master. Whatever had attracted Bligh's name to Cook as a likely candidate for Master, it surely had something to do with his aptitude even as a midshipman for navigation and cartography. Perhaps Cook saw something of his younger self in the unknown midshipman's style. One thing is certain; Cook on this voyage had several eager young men with him who worked hard at laying down the discoveries on their charts, and a great deal of the time of the Commander was spent in supervising rather than doing the cartography himself. This relieved him of a great deal of strain. There is evidence that by this time he was feeling the effects of his almost constant exploring since 1768. For one thing, his temper was sharper than ever before. He flew into rages frequently, and gesticulated so passionately while in a rage that his men referred to these sessions by the Tahitian expression, *heiva*, the name for a native dance then common in the islands, which was characterised by the agitation of the performers.

Cook may well have been a skilful leader of men, but he maintained discipline with judicious doses of the cat. Flogging was a common enough punishment in the eighteenth-century navy, but the extent of it could vary from ship to ship. Captain Hugh Pigot of the *Hermione* and its officers flogged their men so hard and so often that they mutinied and killed him and other officers in 1797 (Pope, 1963). The 'notorious' Captain Bligh only managed to have eleven floggings on his *Bounty* in its fourteen months' voyage; Cook topped sixty floggings in a couple of years (Beaglehole, 1967). This is not to say that Cook was personally responsible for each flogging. Men were reported for punishment by Lieutenants and warrant officers, and the Captain would seldom intervene except in cases of doubt. So Cook was hardly a soft commander; he could be fair, but he could sometimes be outrageous rather than just. On this Third Voyage he ordered an islander thief who had been caught stealing to have not just his hair shaved but also his ears cut off. This was a different man from the Cook who, on the Second Voyage, had decided against punishing Maori cannibals after they had murdered and mutilated some of his men (see Manwaring, 1931, pp. 40-6; Beaglehole, 1974, pp. 519-20).

It would have been surprising, after the experience that Cook had gained on his previous voyages, if he had not regarded himself as fully qualified to deal with all situations that could arise between his men and the islanders or the Indians on the North American continent. He had seen how the firing of the ship's guns or the marines' muskets, or even a few fireworks, terrorised the islanders and ensured their submission, or more correctly their deference, on the occasions when it was needed. Even if his own example was not sufficient, he had the example of Captain Wallis in the *Dolphin*, which visited Matavai Bay in Tahiti in 1768 and engaged in a battle with the Tahitians (for an account of Wallis's experiences, see Furneaux, 1960, pp. 52-77). This confidence, as we shall see, probably played an important part in the events leading to his death.

Cook's officers on the Third Voyage were in the main well known to him; they had sailed with him before and knew the Pacific well. What kind of men were they by the time they reached Hawaii? Only a concise sketch of them can be given here. More detailed assessments of their characters can be found in Beaglehole (1974).

The second-in-command and captain of the *Discovery* was Captain Charles Clerke, thirty-six years old, from Weathersfield in Essex. He was slowly dying of consumption. He most likely caught TB while in the debtor's prison, ironically not for money he owed but for money he had pledged against his brother's debts. His brother, Sir John Clerke, had removed himself from his creditors by voyaging to the East Indies, and when plans for Cook's Third Voyage were made public, with Clerke listed as captain of the *Discovery*, the creditors applied for their money in case he too escaped them. Clerke was committed to jail until he paid. He was still there when Cook departed in the *Resolution* for South Africa, leaving instructions for Clerke to catch up with him when he got out of jail. When Clerke was eventually able to 'outsail the Israelites', as he put it in a letter to Sir Joseph Banks (5 July 1776: see *Historical Records of New South Wales*, first series, vol. i, p.413), he dashed to Portsmouth, took command of the *Discovery* and headed after Cook into the Atlantic. Clerke had sailed on Cook's previous voyages and also with Commodore Byron, the grandfather of the poet, in the *Dolphin* in its circumnavigation of the world in 1764-6 (see Gallagher, 1964; Shankland, 1975). By the time the ships reached Hawaii in 1799, Clerke was weakened by his illness and rapidly failing. This may have had a bearing on what happened at Kealakekua Bay.

First Lieutenant under Cook in the *Resolution* was John Gore, in his late forties and a native of America, then still, but only just, a British colony. He was an extremely experienced Pacific voyager: he had sailed on both Byron's and Wallis's expeditions to the Pacific and circumnavigations of the globe and also on Cook's First Voyage. By this alone he was an admirable First Lieutenant to have on board. The Second Lieutenant was the talented James King, in his mid-twenties, from Lancashire. His naval background was extraordinary in comparison with that of his colleagues. His family was well placed to assist him with 'interest' ashore and this, combined with his natural talents in navigation and astronomy, brought him promotion to Lieutenant at the early age of twenty-one. He then left the sea for a while and studied in Paris and Oxford like the son of a gentleman. Cook's voyage marked King's return to the sea, and with his abilities in astronomy and his Lieutenantcy he was a sensible choice for the expedition. He could work in the dual role of Scientific and Naval Officer. His personal conflict with Bligh during the voyage was not altogether surprising as they would have been in competition with each other.

The character of John Williamson, who was Third Lieutenant on the *Resolution*, is difficult to assess. That he was tetchy when differences arose over the appropriate conduct for a situation we know from those parts of his Log that survive today. He probably still carried a grudge against Cook for their argument over the shooting of a Hawaiian on the first landfall in January 1778. Cook was angry that a Hawaiian had been killed in a scuffle, though Williamson, at least in his ms. Log and Proceedings, went to some length to show that far from being reckless with his firearm he had been more careful than Cook normally was, that he personally abhorred the need to shoot the man, and that only his most persistent and insistent orders to the crews of the boats with him prevented them from firing indiscriminately at the Hawaiians. Among the men he mentioned as wishing to fire when the scuffle broke out were Edgar, Master of the *Discovery*, and William Bligh, Master of the *Resolution*. As a result of the disagreement with Cook over the incident, Williamson claims he requested Cook that 'he never to send me on duty where I could not act from reason & the dictates of my own Conscience' (Beaglehole, 1955-69, p.1349).

Another of Williamson's differences with Cook occurred and was logged in 1777, two years before Hawaii. (There may have been many others but his surviving Log is not complete.) This time it was over Cook's 'strange conduct' regarding the recovery of Williamson's musket, which had been stolen (along with Bligh's) on shore at one of the Tonga Islands. Williamson accuses Cook 'of privately telling the local Tongan chief not to return the stolen musket. This incensed Williamson as the musket in question was his personal property and also a fine piece of workmanship. Williamson wrote, bitterly: 'If a small nail was stolen from Captn Cook, the thief if taken was most severely punished, if of a little more consequence than a nail, then the Chiefs were immediately seized until the things stolen were return'd; I was much more affected by such arbitrary proceedings, than with the loss of my gun, although it was great, I could have no redress' (ibid., pp. 1342-3).

It is of some significance that the events at Kealakekua Bay combined these two questions: the morality of shedding the blood of an islander and the proper response to the theft of ship's property. If, as seems likely, Williamson maintained his resentment at his commander's disregard for his interests, it follows that Cook's choice of Williamson as rear-guard reserve on the morning of his death was foolhardy.

The next man in the line of command on the *Resolution* was William Bligh. Something of the small-group tensions throughout the voyage can be gleaned from Bligh's remarks about some of his colleagues. Bligh made many comments (76 in all) on a copy of Cook and King's official account of the Third Voyage published in 1784. In particular Bligh singles out Lieutenant King, Lieutenant of Marines Molesworth Phillips and Lieutenant Henry Roberts for criticism. Some of these comments will be discussed later. He criticises Phillips in several places. In the first volume he jibes at an exhibition of musket exercises put on by the marines. Cook had ordered them to go through their exercises and also to set off some fireworks. This exhibition was accompanied by the playing of the fife and drum and french horns. According to Cook's account (possibly tidied up by Lieutenant King) it was 'executed tolerably well'. Bligh's marginal note reads: '[A m]ost ludicrous perfor[man]ce for the Marine Officer [was as] incapable of making [his] Men go through their [exerci]se as C. Cook's Mus[ician]s or Musick was [ill] adapted'.[1] Further on, when King writes about the events at Kealakekua Bay, Bligh turns on Phillips once again: 'This person, who was never of any real service the whole Voyage, or did anything but eat and Sleep, was a great Croney of C. King's, and he has taken care not to forget, altho' it is very laughable to those who knew the Characters.'

Lieutenant Molesworth Phillips, the butt of Bligh's criticism, was Irish and in his early twenties. His record was undistinguished at this time, and he never advanced very far in his chosen career. He had gone into the marines on the advice of Sir Joseph Banks and had no military experience prior to the voyage. It is generally agreed that his marines were a sloppy lot. Their inexperience and indiscipline made their own contribution to events when they were called out to earn their keep as Cook's guard. Clearly there was little love lost between Bligh and Phillips, and in later years, after the *Bounty*, Phillips worked hard to turn Sir Joseph Banks against Bligh (see Kennedy, 1978). Phillips was to marry James Burney's sister (Burney was on the *Discovery*) and this introduced him to London society. His alleged close friendship with Lieutenant King had a lasting effect: King publicly praised Phillips for his conduct during the fatal attack on Cook, and as this was published in the official account it did a great deal for his reputation in Britain. He was able to use this account many years later when applying for a pension.

James Burney, the First Lieutenant on the *Discovery*, was twenty-nine and the son of Charles Burney, a successful and talented musician who was courted by the top society of the period. This gave Burney many openings for his chosen career in the navy, and indeed it was his family's interest that placed his name before Lord Sandwich with a view to accompanying Cook on the Third Voyage. He had been on the Second Voyage as Second Lieutenant in the *Adventure* under Captain Furneaux, and this had been arranged after Captain Cook

[1] Brackets indicate where Gould (1928b) has suggested possible letters and words to fill in the gaps caused by an over-zealous bookbinder. See p.94.

(or Lieutenant Cook as he was at that time) was entertained at the Burneys' one evening. As Burney had been appointed in the intervening period to a combat fleet off the North American coast, it required high-level approaches to get him transferred to discovery duties with Cook's Third Voyage. Burney's advance in the navy did not depend entirely on his family – that would be an altogether unfair and inaccurate assertion – because on this voyage and subsequently he proved to be a talented seaman and navigator. He retired a Vice-Admiral. He remained a life-long friend of William Bligh and was to edit Bligh's famous account of the mutiny on the *Bounty* published in 1792 (Manwaring, 1931, pp. 200-1; du Rietz, 1962).

The Second Lieutenant was John Rickman, of whom little is known except that he remained a lieutenant for his entire naval career. It has been suggested, somewhat tenuously, that he was related to the Speaker of the House of Commons, John Rickman (Manwaring, 1931, p.215). If so, this suggests some substantial background. What we do know of him is confined to his actions on the morning of Cook's death, and there are veiled suggestions in some of the accounts that he precipitated the assault on Cook by his conduct over a mile away at the other side of the Bay. I will discuss the credibility of these later. We might note here that Bligh's marginal notes strongly imply that Rickman was not to blame for what happened.

The Master of the *Discovery*, Thomas Edgar, also played a role in the events that follow, and we have two sources of information about him: first, his own surviving ms. Log. Large parts of this account appear to be copied out of other people's. The other source is a comment written by one of his subsequent colleagues, James Gardiner, many years later when Edgar had made the rank of Lieutenant: 'The first lieutenant, Edgar, was another strange and unaccountable being. He had sailed round the world with Cook, and was master of the ship Captain Clerke commanded. He was a good sailor and navigator, or rather had been, for he drank very hard, so as to entirely ruin his constitution. He and the captain often quarrelled, particularly at night' (Hamilton and Laughton, eds., 1906, p.165; see also Sherton, 1937). Williamson, in his Log, makes at least two critical remarks about Edgar. There is no doubt that the standard of discipline on board the *Discovery* was slacker than that on the *Resolution*.

Among the junior officers on the *Discovery* there were three who left their mark on naval history at later dates, though only one of them was directly involved in the death of Cook. George Vancouver, midshipman, was severely beaten up by Hawaiians the night before Cook died. Vancouver went on after the Third Voyage to establish his own reputation as an explorer, discoverer, cartographer and informal ambassador in the Pacific in a long voyage to the north-west coast of America; he made some important diplomatic advances with the Hawaiians and further investigated the circumstances of Captain Cook's death (see his published account of the voyage: Vancouver, 1798). Vancouver in Canada is named after him. Edward Riou, another midshipman, was present at Kealakekua Bay but is not known to have played a direct part. He certainly had something special in him as a naval officer; he became famous for his role in saving the sinking *Guardian* which had been holed by an iceberg off South Africa, and for his short but intimate relationship with Nelson at the bloody battle of Copenhagen in 1801, where he was killed in action (Kennedy, 1978; Pope, 1970). Senior to these men was Nathaniel Portlock, Master's Mate of the *Discovery*. He made his own voyage round the world a few years later (Portlock, 1789) and served as second in command to William Bligh in his Second Breadfruit Voyage, after the *Bounty* mutiny.

There were several others on the voyage whose writings and opinions I will discuss in the course of the following chapters. David Samwell, Assistant Surgeon on the *Resolution*, made an important contribution to the history of Cook's death (Samwell, 1786); William Ellis, Assistant Surgeon on the *Discovery*, did likewise (Ellis, 1782). William Bayly, astronomer of the *Discovery*, John Webber, the voyage's official artist, Alexander Home, Master's Mate of the *Discovery*, and James Trevenen, midshipman on the *Resolution*, all made individual contributions to the record of the voyage (Bayly, 1782; Home, 1779); and Trevenen annotated his own copy of King's volume of the official account of the voyage (Lloyd and Anderson, 1959).

These, then, were some of the men with Cook in Kealakekua Bay. Most of the 180 or so seamen who sailed on the voyage have not left any record of their roles and the part they played at Kealakekua. But boats were manned in the bay and guns were fired by these anonymous figures. Over 60 men fought on the morai that morning and only a handful can be identified. What kind of men they were we can only guess. But in a way it does not matter too much that we are ignorant of their characters and abilities; Cook died mainly as a result of his own and his officers' failings rather than those of the men they commanded.

II

The Return of Lono

When Cook's two ships hove into sight of an undiscovered island in the vast emptiness of the north Pacific, on the afternoon of 18 January 1778, more than a year before his death, they brought the people of the Hawaiian islands into contact with another part of the world for the first time since the Hawaiians left the Society Isles years (perhaps centuries) before (Buck, 1945). The folk memory of the Hawaiians kept alive their origins at least as far back as Tahiti: the Hawaiian language was similar to that of the Tahitians, and they used the word Tahiti to refer both to their origins and to foreign lands. Of the outside world they had no idea whatsoever.[1] The arrival of the two ships required an explanation within the confines of the religious beliefs of the people. This the priests were to provide in the myth of the god known as Lono.

When Cook stepped ashore at Waimea Bay on the island of Atooi (now known as Kauai), one of the western islands in the Hawaiian group, the people on the beach fell prostrate before him. The Hawaiians may have done this out of fear, since Williamson had already killed one of them. But they had not prostrated themselves for Williamson. It was to Cook that they directed their reverence. At this moment the people ashore were without their chiefs and priests, and their reaction was probably not yet connected with the idea of deification.

On Cook's first visit to Tahiti in 1769, he had gone to some lengths to establish that any venereal disease on the island was there before his ships arrived. He indignantly rejected charges that his own men had brought it, though the ships' medical records show that many of his men had it. On this visit to the Hawaiian islands he wanted

[1] Some authors have suggested that Cook was not the first European to visit the Hawaiian islands: see Rev. William Ellis (1974). Beaglehole (1974, p.580; 1955-69, vol. 3, pp. 285-6) dismissed the idea that Spanish ships visited them before Cook.

desperately to keep his men away from intimate contact with the inhabitants, to prevent accusations at a later date that his people had spread venereal disease among these islands, which as far as he could determine had not been visited by Europeans before. To this end he ordered that all men with the 'fowl disease' were to be confined to the ship, no women were to be allowed on board and no sexual relations were to be permitted ashore. By keeping everybody on board at night he hoped to lessen the chance of disobedience to his orders (Beaglehole, 1955-69, vol. 3, pp. 265-6; I have used this edition of Cook's Journals for much of this chapter). But the best laid plans of mice and men ... One thing Cook could not hope to control was the weather. On 29 January Cook was lying off Oneeheow, as wind and current had made the anchorage at Waimea Bay dangerous. He sent Lieutenant Gore and twenty men ashore to look for water and supplies. A storm blew up and the result was that 'the very thing happened that I had above all others wished to prevent' – the shore party spent two days and nights off the ships and among the people. Cook's regulations about sexual intercourse with the locals had been breached before and it may be assumed that they were again. On 2 February 1778 he took his ships on a northern course, having named his discovery the Sandwich Islands, after Lord Sandwich, a name they kept until the middle of the nineteenth century when they took the name of the largest island in the group and became known as Hawaii.

After a fruitless search for a northern passage to Europe, though a far from fruitless survey of the coasts was made, Cook set course on 26 October for the Sandwich Islands. He decided to use the winter for further surveying of his new discovery before returning to the north for another attempt on the ice packs. He approached the Hawaiian group from the east with a view to deciding whether there were other islands in the group beyond the five he had seen the previous January. Landfall was made at Mowee (Maui) on 26 November 1778, exactly a month after leaving the north.

The return to Hawaii raised the old problems of discipline. Arguments, accidents, sudden flare-ups of temper, ignorance and avarice all threatened the broad interests of the mission as Cook saw it. He posted regulations as usual to cover the conduct of the men while ashore and when dealing with the local inhabitants on board (for whenever the ships came within a few miles of the shore, scores of boats came out laden with trade and women). Women and firearms gave him his biggest problems. Lost firearms provoked trouble and he forbade anybody to carry firearms out of the ships, including the officers. Williamson and Bligh, it will be remembered, had had theirs stolen in Tonga. But the biggest concern that Cook felt was, again, the moral one of the responsibility for the 'fatal disease' getting among the 'Innocent people'.

His efforts to avoid charges of spreading venereal disease were certainly well-intended. But Cook's later image as a 'born leader', beloved by his men who obeyed him without question, is at variance with the real situation on his ships at that time. There are signs, particularly during this second visit to Hawaii, that Cook was not as much in control of his men as later biographers have romanticised. There were over 180 men on board the *Resolution* and *Discovery*, and they certainly did not regard the issues of social responsibility in the same light as their Commander. They might be disciplined in the naval sense of running up the rigging or manning the yards, and they might always be deferential when near an officer, but this is not the same thing as observing irksome rules that frustrated their more sensual appetites, particularly if they could find willing accomplices out of sight of authority.

Cook's rules regarding women were not posted with an outraged sense of prudery on his part. He knew the realities of life in Polynesia as well as any. But his rules do have a sense of desperation about them which ironically made them all the easier to ignore. As at Atooi, women were not to be allowed into the ships; seamen who brought them on boats 'without the Captain's permission' were to be punished; men having venereal disease who had sexual relations with Hawaiian women were to be 'severely' punished and nobody with the disease, or even suspected of having it by the Surgeons, was to be allowed ashore. The crews were assembled and the regulations read out (Cook, 1779b). Cook even made a special plea for their observance in a speech to the men on the *Resolution* (King, 1784). When eventually the men got ashore, however, the regulations were forgotten, much to the dismay of Cook. He seems eventually to have accepted the consequences with a certain fatalism, which supports the suggestion that he was weary and pessimistic at this stage of the voyage.

While they were off Mowee a distinguished visitor came on board, though his distinction was not fully appreciated at the time. He appeared weak, though this may have been exaggerated by the fact that his servants carried him everywhere for reasons of protocol, and he had the tell-tale marks of an addicted kava drinker: his skin was scabby and his eyes bloodshot. His name was Terreeoboo. To the dismay of the crew, Cook did not anchor the ships at this inviting island. In fact, Terreeoboo himself came from the larger island called Hawaii that was said to be to the south, and he was engaged in a local war at Mowee which might have precluded a proper welcome if the seamen had gone ashore. The track of the *Resolution* in the next five weeks was a long meandering course down the east side of Hawaii, alternatively approaching the land and then backing off again. For the men, within sight of the nearest they were ever to get to paradise, the business was frustrating, and they were in an aggressive mood. The only thing the crew wanted to know was when they were going to get ashore. Even the most angelic of souls would have been demoralised with the progress of the voyage, especially after the rigours and deprivation of the months spent up in the higher, colder and bleaker latitudes.

On 7 December 1778, in one of the approaches to the coast of the island of Hawaii, Cook traded for meat, fruit and roots from the many canoes that came off that day. In the afternoon the ships got under way and once again the crew saw the coast dropping away without a spell of shore leave. Two issues sparked off trouble. The first is somewhat incredible: the men were still on sea rations instead of full rations for landfall. For some reason Cook had not, as was customary, altered the rations when his ships came in sight of land. An eyewitness to the scene, Midshipman John Watts, has left us a report of the incident (Beaglehole, 1955-69, vol. 3, pp. 479-80):

the people remonstrated with the Captn by Letter at same time mentioning the scanty Allowance of Provisions serv'd them, which they thought might be increas'd where there was such Plenty & that bought for mere trifles. This Morning therefore the Captn order'd the Hands aft, & told them, that it was the first time He had heard any thing relative to the shortness of the Allowance, that he thought they had had the same Quantity usually serv'd them at the other Islands, that if they had not enough, they should have more & that had He known it sooner, it should have been rectified.

It is extraordinary that Cook did not know what rations his crew was on, given his well-known interest in their diet as an antidote to scurvy. Beaglehole suggests that he forgot, which again suggests a different

Cook from the one of the previous voyages (Beaglehole, 1974, p.641).

The other issue, about which the men also complained in their letter, was the perennial one of something new in the diet. In this case it was beer, brewed on Cook's orders from Hawaiian sugar cane. The men thought it injurious to their health. This was a suggestion likely to cut him to the quick, for his whole life as a commander had been dedicated, in his opinion, to finding nourishing food for his men; it was for this that he had won the Royal Society's Copley Gold Medal in 1776.[2] He had noted that 'every innovation whatever tho ever so much to their advantage is sure to meet with the highest disapprobation from Seamen' (Beaglehole, 1955-69, p.479). Indeed, he had flogged men who refused his 'new fangled' food. Midshipman Watts continues his account:

He likewise understood He said they would not drink the Decoction of Sugar Cane imagining it prejudicial to their Healths, he told them it was something extraordinary they should suppose the Decoction unwholesome when they could steal the Sugar Cane & eat it raw without Scruple he continued to tell them that if they did not chuse to drink the Decoction he could not help it, they would be the Sufferers as they should have Grog every other day provided they drank the Sugar Cane, but if not the Brandy Cask should be struck down into the Hold & they might content themselves with Water, intimating to them that he did not chuse to keep turning and working among the Isles without having som Profit.[3] He gave them 24 Hours to consider of it.

It is not known what effect this injunction had on his weary men. The brandy cask was sent down the hold, but for how long is likewise not known. According to Watts, the cooper, William Griffiths, also received a dozen lashes for issuing sour Hawaiian beer. The crew were told by Cook that he regarded them as 'mutinous' and that 'in future they might not expect the least indulgence from him' (Watts, ms. Journal and Proceedings).

A few days later, after some of the *Resolution*'s rigging gave way under strain, he made a relatively outspoken criticism in his Journal of the general quality of the naval stores issued to him for the voyage

---

[2] For an interesting, if eulogistic, account of Cook's contribution to nourishment at sea, see Villiers (1969).

[3] The 'profit' was the saving of the stores allowance if the men could be persuaded to drink beer instead of the official ration of grog. As Captain, Cook was also Purser, and the saving went into his own pocket.

(Beaglehole, 1955-69, vol. 3, pp. 481-2). This was, in effect, a criticism of his friend and sponsor, Sir Hugh Palliser, then Comptroller of the Navy and responsible for the work of the naval dockyards. Palliser was later to have the offending passage edited in the official publication (Beaglehole, 1974, p.644). Again, this kind of behaviour was unusual for Cook, who had always been circumspect in his personal dealings with authority. He was probably only articulating in this particular entry what his officers and men were saying in the privacy of the ship while trying to put right the damage to the rigging. Out of sympathy with his men at this point over the home-brewed beer, exasperated by technical difficulties (both ships were leaking), anxious about the responsibility for spreading venereal disease but knowing he could not keep the ships at sea indefinitely, Cook at this point could only submit to the inevitable and try to restore his bonds with his men by quickly finding a safe and commodious place to anchor in.

After beating round the eastern side of Hawaii, with the added problem of losing contact with the *Discovery* for twelve days, Cook began to search for an anchorage. The decision to end the sea patrolling was made when the *Resolution* and *Discovery* came together again on 6 January 1779. It was not until 15 January that a possible anchorage was sighted, on the west coast of the island of Hawaii. Cook sent Bligh to survey the small indentation, hardly a bay, in the coast and to report on the state of the local water supplies and also the general demeanour of the inhabitants. The latter, however, required no verbal report from Bligh, for as the ships stood off waiting for Bligh's survey, something like a thousand canoes came out to the ships, with an estimated crowd, in them and the water around the ships, of ten thousand people. This was something completely unexpected and astonishing. The Hawaiians brought food and gifts with them in their canoes and not a weapon of any kind was seen. This was a royal, even god-like, welcome.

They could not possibly all have been local inhabitants of the bay, and indeed they were not. Cook's party had been sailing round the island for several weeks and news of their movements, their friendly trade, their magnificent ships and strange ways had been spread far and wide by excited Hawaiians. By the time the ships approached the bay they had attracted thousands of curious sightseers and followers. The fact that they chose this bay was sombre in its implications, for it had a special significance to the people of Hawaii. It was known as

Karakakooa (Kealakekua) Bay, which meant 'pathway to the gods'. Cook was accidentally fulfilling Hawaiian religious prophesies (Daws, 1968a; Bushnell, 1971). From now on there were two parallel dramas being enacted (three if we count the headlong pursuit of women by the sex-starved crews). On one level Cook was enacting the Hawaiian legend of the return of Lono, a mythical figure from the lost aeons of Hawaiian history who they believed would one day return from the sea. On another level, Cook was replenishing his supplies, repairing his ships and making observations as a European discoverer and scientist. The dramas incorporated the same actors, the same lines and the same plots, but the audiences, Hawaiian and European, viewed and understood them entirely differently.

The missionary Hiram Bingham took down a version of the legend of Lono from a Hawaiian who told the story and related it to Cook's arrival (Bingham, 1855, p.32; Rev. William Ellis, 1974, pp. 134-5, has a nearly identical version):

In very ancient time, Lono dwelt at Kealakekua with his *wahine* [wife] Kaikilanialiiopuna. They dwelt together under the precipice. A man ascended the *pali* and called to the woman. 'O Kaikilanialiiopuna, may one dare approach you – your paramour – Ohea the soldier? This to join – that to flee – you and I to sleep.' Lono hearing, was angry and smote his *wahine*, and Kaikilanialiiopuna died. He took her up, bore into the temple and there left her. He lamented over her and travelled around Hawaii, Maui, Molakai, Oahu and Kuaai boxing with those he met. The people exclaimed, Behold Lono, greatly crazed! Lono replied, 'I am crazed for her – I am frantic on account of her love.' He left the islands and went to a foreign land in a triangular canoe, called *Paimalu*. Kaikilanialiiopuna came to life again, and travelled all round the islands searching after her husband. The people demanded of her, 'What is your husband's name?' She replied, 'Lono.' 'Was that crazy husband yours?' 'Aye mine.' Kaikilanialiiopuna then sailed by a canoe to a foreign land. On arrival of ships the people exclaimed, 'Lo this is Lono! Here come Lono!'

The gist of the legend was that Lono went away to sea but would return. Hawaiian gods were grotesque representations of the human form in wood, but Lono's representations were comparatively simple – a small head on a long pole. His former residence at Kealakekua Bay gave the area some religious significance (Daws, 1968a). At the time of Cook's visit Kakooa, one of the two villages, was mainly devoted to the priests and their entourage (*Kakooa* meant 'place of worship'), and was proud

of its morai (or *heiau*), a temple structure discussed below. One of the
interesting aspects of the legend was the annual festival of *makahiki*, in
which Lono was represented in his boat by large pieces of draped
white cloths, not unlike a ship's sails. The festival lasted three weeks,
and Cook's ships approached the island of Hawaii during this time.
Canoes came out for trade bearing what looked like white streamers,
which the Europeans naturally took to be symbols of truce, peace and
safe conduct. In fact they were the symbols of Lono. Conversely, the
Hawaiians had an explanation for the sight of the massive ships with
their enormous white sails: it was Lono returned. No doubt this
tentative conclusion was reinforced by the local priests: the timely
fulfilment of the prophecy enhanced their status. The competition
between secular and spiritual power, represented by the chiefs and the
priests respectively, was of great importance at this time in Hawaii.
The arrival of the Europeans gave an explosive twist to this age-old
and universal conflict.[4]

The news of Lono's return spread throughout the island, and the
coincidence of his return with his festival gave the news an enormous
emotional impetus. Cook's welcome in the bay was an expression of
the Hawaiians' excitement (see Daws, 1968a). This continued
throughout the stay of the ships. When Bligh returned to the *Resolution*
with his detailed survey complete and the report on the fresh water
available at one of the villages, the choice of the bay for the anchorage
was inevitable. Everybody was overjoyed. Cook was forced to give up
his hopeless quest to keep his men away from the women; the women
were as determined as the men to get together, and get together they
did. By this time Cook had bowed to the inevitable. He believed his
men had spread the disease from the two nights ashore the year
before; he recorded observations of something like a venereal
complaint on some of the people who came on board at Kealakekua,
and wondered whether it could spread so fast (Beaglehole, 1955-69,
p.474; Riou, ms. Log).

During this first visit to Kealakekua, Cook was initiated into an

---

[4] The old Hawaiian religion was eventually destroyed in the domestic struggle to create a
single state out of Hawaii and the surrounding islands. King Kamehameha (Tamehameha), the
first sovereign, was at Kealakekua Bay at the time of Cook's visit, participated in the affray and
was wounded. He later fought for many years to unite Hawaii and defeat his opponents, and
was greatly assisted in his campaigns by the acquisition of European firearms and ships. His
heir, Rihoriho, completed the secularisation of Hawaii in 1819, defeating his rivals who
supported the priesthood and the old religion (Ellis, 1974, pp. 122-8).

obscure, and at times revolting, ceremony by the priests on the morai. The morai was built of thousands of stones and was an impressive construction in a country in which most buildings were of wood and straw. It stood about fifteen feet high and was about sixty feet wide by one hundred and twenty feet long. A partially reconstructed morai can be seen on the same site in Kealakekua Bay today (1978); it is a formidable structure giving a commanding view of the surrounding area. On it were several wooden idols, and it was surrounded by a wooden fence. The ceremony was conducted by a priest called Koa, who was assisted by a younger priest called Kaireekeea. The entire ritual was lost on the Europeans, Cook, King and Bayly. The only constant thing they could capture from the chanting in the unknown language was the single word 'orono' (or Lono). People prostrated themselves everywhere, as they had done the year before at Atooi, and this time Cook was always accompanied by attendants chanting 'Lono'. Neither Cook nor anybody else from the ships could understand what was going on. But if it meant friendly relations and trouble-free intercourse, why should the Europeans complain? Cook's lack of effort to understand the Hawaiians' response made him vulnerable to criticism later from the missionaries. Of course, these men of virtue and principle had another axe to grind and Cook's fate gave them excellent material for a sermon.[5]

When Terreeoboo returned from the war in Mowee he exchanged many gifts with Cook. The priests, however, were clearly in the ascendant at that moment. Their power to institute the *tapu* (taboo) was of immense assistance to Cook's men. It cleared land next to the morai for the ship's observatories (under the charge of Lieutenant King); it kept clear a part of a beach for the ships' boats to use; and, just before Terreeoboo's return, it cleared the entire bay of people, as was the custom on the arrival of the local King. For two weeks the near-idyllic relationship blossomed. But for some reason the welcome began to wear thin.

There have been several explanations of this. One is that the drain on the local food supplies of near on two hundred men eating their fill every day, not to mention the several thousand Hawaiian visitors nearby, was undermining the local economy. Lieutenant King

---

[5] Bingham (1855), p.34, is an example of those who directed abusive sermons at Cook's memory; he refers to Cook as a 'worm'.

thought this was the prime reason for the unsubtle hints to the Europeans to leave. 'It was ridiculous enough,' he wrote (King, 1784), 'to see them stroking the sides, and patting the bellies of the sailors (who had certainly much improved in the sleekness of their looks, during our short stay in the island) and telling them, partly by signs, and partly by words, that it was time for them to go.' A year previously, Cook had only stayed a few days at Atooi and Oneeheow, but he was at Kealakekua two weeks. What interpretation the Hawaiians put on this we do not know, but it may not have been unconnected with the secular-priestly tensions. The priests were lording it while Cook was there, and the old King or his subordinate chiefs may have had enough of this, thinking that the quicker they got rid of Lono the quicker they could reassert their power.

Another explanation has to do with the alleged desecration of the morai by Cook's men. This implies that the moves to get rid of Cook came from the priests. The incident arose from the need of firewood for the ships. Normally Cook would have arranged to trade for trees to be felled, offering payment in the usual currency of iron nails. For some reason, on this occasion the wood party was sent to the wooden fence round the morai. Lieutenant King was ordered by Cook to obtain from Koa, the priest, permission to dismantle the fence and take it aboard the vessels (Beaglehole, 1974, p.655). According to King, Koa did not seem at all displeased with this suggestion, nor did the men experience any difficulty in acquiring the fence, and some of the wooden idols as well. It is difficult now to know what actually happened, or how this action appeared to the local inhabitants. Ledyard states quite explicitly in his book that the Hawaiians were shocked at the vandalism on the morai and that they resisted it furiously. He wrote: 'By this time a considerable concourse of the natives had assembled under the walls of the Morai, where we were heaving the wood down, and were very outrageous, and even hove the wood and images back as we threw them down, and I cannot think what prevented them from proceeding to greater lengths, however it so happened that we got the whole into the boats and safely on board' (Ledyard, 1783, p.137). Which version is the truth? Lieutenant King did the negotiating with Koa, who may well have been anxious to go along with anything that Lono wanted in order to keep in good standing with the deity who had brought such prestige to his work. He may have assumed that Lono wanted the images and the fence for his own morai on the ship. Ledyard on the other hand clearly was one of the work party engaged in collecting the wood (though it is a strange duty for a Corporal of Marines).

The controversy over this incident continued throughout the nineteenth century. A Hawaiian historian did not think the matter was that important. He pointed out that the wooden images set up outside the morai 'were not restricted (*tapu*) for use as oven fuel' (Thurm, 1926, pp. 56-7; Dibble, 1909, p.25). The local people, he said, sometimes used them for firewood. Kamakau (1935) made the point that Kawelo, a warrior king, prepared for one of his wars on Kauai by consecrating the morai of Puelu at Waianee. After the service he commanded the wood of the fence and also the images to be taken for firewood. If Cook as Lono took the wood from the morai, perhaps he was seen as promising a war on somebody; if so, the inhabitants would be glad to see him go, as they would then be sure that they themselves were not his target.

Whatever the reason for the lessening of friendship, on 4 February 1779 Cook took the ships out of the bay. The send-off was as spectacular as the arrival; gifts were showered on the crews, either to hurry them away or to hasten them back. Lono had left them. The King could get back to governing his people again, collecting the tribute and ruling through his chiefs. The priests could get back to their calling as spiritual advisers. The women, some of them probably pregnant, could return to their husbands and families. It must have come as a shock six days later to see the great ships enter the bay again. Lono had only four days left to live.

III

Edgar's Folly

Cook had been forced to return to Kealakekua by circumstances outside his control. After they left the bay on 4 February the weather had deteriorated into squalls, heavy seas and eventually gales. A vain search was made for a harbour. The nearest they came to an anchorage was at Toe-yah-yah (Kawaihae), but Bligh's thorough survey confirmed its unsuitability. During his survey, even local canoes got into difficulty with the rising seas, and Bligh rescued two men and a woman from their sinking canoe. Other canoes were rescued by the ships. During the night of 7 February the *Resolution*'s foremast was badly sprung – it had already had temporary repairs at Nootka Sound (on modern Vancouver Island) – and it was imperative that the mast be repaired once again. This was a task that was easier if the mast could be taken on shore. The choice for Cook was between continuing the search in uncertain and possibly dangerous weather for a suitable harbour either on Hawaii or Mowee, or returning to the relative security of Kealakekua Bay. The arguments against the former choice were that there was no certainty of finding a suitable place and that a continuation of the gales could endanger the *Resolution* in its weakened state. The argument against a return to Kealakekua was that Cook knew he had outstayed his welcome there. But faced with a choice of evils he had to take the one that ensured the safety of his ship, even at the cost of political goodwill. Accordingly the helms were swung round and the ships headed back the way they had come.

The ships arrived at Kealakekua Bay again on 11 February. On Bligh's chart the course of the *Resolution* from Toe-yah-yah Bay is shown, with the ship's near miss of the shoals at the south end of the bay clearly marked. Much has been made of the absence of people in the bay on the ship's return (Maclean, 1972, p.178; Hough, 1972, pp. 39-40; King, 1784). Some part of this is, of course, a retrospective rationalisation. The absence of people can have a quite innocent explanation at least as credible as the more usual sinister one that the people had left the bay in anger at the ships' return. The ships had left on 4 February and the thousands of Hawaiians who had arrived from all over the island to see the strangers had returned to their villages, from which they had been absent for a week or more. The foul weather kept many people inside their houses, and the earlier procession of inhabitants following the progress of the ships along the coast had not occurred this time. Also, King Terreeoboo had left his residence at the village of Kowrowa at the north end of Kealakekua and gone inland. As was his custom, he had ordered the priests to place a *tapu* on the bay until his return. This would be more than enough to make all the visiting Hawaiians leave the area as fast as they could and would also prevent them returning except with the greatest hesitation and circumspection. Breaches of a *tapu* not only enraged the gods, they could make the transgressor a candidate for severe retribution from the chiefs, particularly when the short leet for human sacrifices was being prepared. In some respects the absence of people made Cook's mission easier; the foremast could be got out and on shore without the interference and the distraction of thousands of friendly visitors.

The priests who lived in the bay immediately came to the assistance of the seamen by placing another *tapu* on the area near the morai for the convenience of the carpenters and marines to conduct their work. An observatory was set up so that the astronomers could take the opportunity (seldom missed by Cook) to carry out some scientific work. Everything was moving smoothly and the prospects looked fair for a speedy repair of the mast. But King Terreeoboo had not yet appeared and it was not known how things stood with him regarding this surprising return. He turned up in the late morning, and according to Lieutenant Burney he 'appeared much dissatisfied' with Cook's return (Beaglehole, 1955-69, vol. 3, p.528). As a dutiful host he went through the civilities, exchanged presents with Cook and then set up his residence at the village of Kowrowa. His presence brought back the Hawaiians and they began to drift in that afternoon and over the next days. The arrivals erected their temporary huts and beached their canoes, and slowly relations between the Hawaiians and the seamen warmed up. But something was different this time.

Who or what was responsible is a matter of conjecture. The hysteria of the earlier visit had changed into a new, and potentially threatening, familiarity. True, friendships were renewed, trading began again and the rounds of diplomatic exchanges between Captains Cook and Clerke and the chiefs and priests gathered momentum. But clearly this was a different kind of visit. For one thing Lono's ship, the *Resolution*, was disabled, and one of its main features was laid out on shore with men doing work on it. Some of the majesty of the ship was lost through the quite ordinary problems of split and rotten wood. Another feature of the situation was the relationship between the Hawaiians and the seamen. This became strained. Some of the Hawaiians clearly did not have the same high regard for their visitors as before. Perhaps some of Terreeoboo's annoyance, alluded to by Burney, was picked up by his subjects, or the arguments among the chiefs about the meaning of this second visit caused speculation, both friendly and sinister, among the ordinary men and women who had returned in the wake of their chiefs. If the chiefs were suspicious it is hardly surprising that their subjects were increasingly haughty, difficult, mischievous and provocative. The troublesome faction seems to have consisted of some of the lesser chiefs and their retinues.

The weakest link in the friendship between Cook's men and the Hawaiians was the *Discovery*. Captain Clerke, we know, was ill with TB and less than fully fit for his job. It had even been suggested, over a year previously, that he should be left behind at Tahiti to convalesce while the ships went north to the Arctic (Burney, 1819, pp. 233-4). His illness must have contributed to some slackness on this ship compared to the *Resolution*, and it would appear that the Hawaiians, bent on trouble, recognised the difference in tautness of discipline and concentrated their depredations accordingly on Clerke's ship.

Clerke reported in his ms. Journal that there was a 'stronger propensity to theft than we had reason to complain of during our former stay; every day produced more numerous and more audacious depredations – today they behaved so ill on board the *Discovery* that I was obliged to order them all out of the ship, which I find was likewise the case on board the *Resolution*, none but the principal people were suffered on board, however we let them lay alongside in their Canoes and amuse themselves as they thought proper'. Audacious they certainly were. One Hawaiian stole the armourer's tongs, but was caught. Clerke was exasperated and ordered the man flogged, and he was duly given forty lashes.

King Terreeoboo visited Clerke and presented him with a splendid Hawaiian cloak and a hog. Earlier, Clerke had traded with Kamehameha (the future King of Hawaii) nine or, in some accounts, seven specially-made long knives in exchange for a Hawaiian feathered cloak. These feathered cloaks were highly prized objects among the Hawaiians, worn only by the highest ranking personages. The Hawaiians were becoming discriminating in their trade, and the earlier near-robbery of provisions in return for ordinary nails (women had even offered sex in return for a nail) was being replaced by more cunning and ambitious bargaining.

Meanwhile, on shore, Lieutenant King was having problems with a watering party. The party came from the *Discovery* under the command of William Hollamby, quartermaster. One of the local chiefs was encouraging a crowd of Hawaiians to annoy the seamen, who were collecting water from a small spring at the cliff side of the village of Kakooa. The ground beside the well rises steeply for several hundred feet, and the Hawaiians were amusing themselves by rolling stones down the hill into the area where the seamen were working. Hollamby asked King for assistance, and eventually King had to go to the spring with an armed marine, at which the crowd desisted from its game. Captain Cook, coincidentally, was inspecting the shore camp at Kakooa at this time, and when King reported to him what had happened Cook told him to 'fire a ball at the offenders' on the 'first' appearance of throwing stones or behaving insolently' (Beaglehole, 1955-69, vol. 3, p.529). This was an important change in British-Hawaiian public relations, and marked a move towards the policy of giving a punitive demonstration of European fire-power to overawe the islanders. In the past, displays of this kind, either harmless fireworks or the more drastic sanction of shooting to kill in a selected incident, had had the intended effect of restoring or establishing in the Polynesians a friendly but submissive attitude towards their visitors. King is quite specific, both here (in his Log) and in a later statement (King, 1784), that Captain Cook made it clear to him on 13 February, the day before the fatal affray, that this was to be the new policy. It came too late, however: although sufficient incidents followed to warrant the use of firearms, it was not possible for one reason or another to use this sanction effectively.

After King Terreeoboo had departed from the *Discovery*, Clerke had another visitor, this time the lesser chief Parea. Clerke entertained him in his cabin while the marines watched the Hawaiians circling the ship in their canoes. But the watch was not careful enough. A Hawaiian got up the side of the *Discovery*, ran across the deck, grabbed the armourer's tongs and a chisel and as quickly jumped overboard again. A canoe was apparently standing by ready to paddle off; it picked him up from the water with his prizes and was moving out of range while the startled guards were getting themselves ready to retaliate.

Clerke rushed from his cabin with Parea behind him and was told what the alarm was about. He ordered the marines to open fire on the rapidly departing canoe, but by this time they were at the limit of the range of the muskets. Clerke ordered his Master, Thomas Edgar, to take the small cutter and give chase. Edgar took with him Midshipman George Vancouver and two seamen, but in his rush to catch the canoe did not stop to take firearms.[1]

Captain Cook was still on shore at this moment with Lieutenant King, and the sound of gunfire and the sight of the commotion drew them to the water's edge to see what was going on. It was clear to them that a delinquent was once again at work, though they were not aware exactly what offence he had committed. The marines were firing from the *Discovery*, and the musket fire signalled that something of importance was at stake. Cook hurried along the shore towards the cove where the canoe was headed. He took Lieutenant King with him and two marines (Beaglehole, 1974, p.664); some accounts mention only one marine, perhaps because they were a corporal and a private and only one was armed with a musket. Whatever it was that the delinquent had done, Cook intended to apprehend him and wait for the *Discovery*'s boat which was giving chase.

Things did not work out as Cook, Clerke or Edgar intended. After Edgar had left the *Discovery* in the cutter to give chase to the thief in the canoe, Parea suggested to Clerke that if he, Parea, went ashore he would be able to settle the matter amicably and regain the stolen property. It seemed a generous offer, though if one believes, as everybody later suspected, that he was the instigator of the theft in the first place, it was more likely a simple ruse to get himself off the ship.

---

[1] I have used Edgar's own ms. Log as the main source for my account of what happened after this. Other accounts follow his account substantially, though they are critical of his actions or differ in minor details (see, e.g., Law's ms. Journal, and Ledyard quoted in Munford 1963a).

Clerke agreed, and Parea immediately got into one of the canoes and paddled for the shore. While Captain Cook and his party were running along the shore-line, his pinnace from the *Resolution*, manned and waiting on the oars, followed him just off shore. This was a natural and automatic thing for the Captain's boat crew to do. Thus, Edgar saw not just the Captain, Lieutenant King and the marines running towards the point where he would beach his cutter, but also the captain's pinnace apparently rowing towards him. This gave his chase even more importance. It was not only ordered by Captain Clerke and accompanied by musket fire, but the commander-in-chief of the voyage, with reinforcements, was on his way to help him, so it must have seemed to Edgar. Certainly his subsequent behaviour was induced by some increased sense of status for him and his mission.

Under the illusion that the captain's pinnace had arms, Edgar continued to row to the shore. The canoe he had been chasing reached a sandy cove before Cook, King and the marines got there, and the offenders ran off into the country behind the beach. Cook and his party gave chase, but relied for directions on some local Hawaiian 'guides' who only pretended to look for the thieves. Edgar, approaching the cove, was met by another canoe which brought to him the stolen tongs, the chisel and the lid of the water cask from the *Discovery*. This latter item had not been missed up to that point. The thieves had obviously abandoned these things in their rush to get away, and their return should have been sufficient to end the matter for the time being, but Edgar decided that restoration was not enough. This was his biggest mistake, especially as he was unarmed. He wanted to seize the thief's canoe and take it back to the ship. To this end he rowed into the cove, followed by the *Resolution*'s pinnace, which beached. Cook's party had already gone inland in pursuit of the thieves.

Edgar and Vancouver jumped ashore, took hold of the canoe and were pushing it into the water when Chief Parea arrived on the scene. Meanwhile the cutter pulled off shore. Parea told Edgar that the canoe he was taking belonged to him and that he was not to remove it. This declaration of ownership of the offending canoe helped implicate Parea in the incident. Edgar persisted in his attempt to launch it into the water. Meanwhile a crowd of Hawaiians had gathered at the cove, drawn there by the musket fire, the shouting and the sight of Lono running into the area. They must have been bewildered at what was going on, but they soon decided that the white men were up to no good, especially when Parea and Edgar started struggling for control of the canoe. Edgar wrote this account in his ms. Log: 'Par-rea came & Hindered me, by taking out one of the paddles and Holding her. I took the paddle from him, he then came up behind me, and while I was putting the Canoe off a second time he Seized on me, when one of the pinnace men, seeing this, up with his Oar & Struck Pa-rea on the Head, at that Inst a Shower of Stones came from about 2 or 3 hundred People on a Rising Ground, & soon after closed on the Pinnace ...'

The Polynesian habit of stone throwing was not just annoying, it was dangerous. The entire bay is still covered today with thousands of stones; they are rough, heavy lumps of lava that come in every shape and size. As they could weigh up to a pound or two, they could severely damage muscle or bone. Edgar, Vancouver and the men in the pinnace took the brunt of the stone-throwing. The pinnace men abandoned their boat, which they had beached, and swam out to some rocks where they were taken on board the cutter. Edgar was unable to follow them, because he could not swim; and Vancouver showed his sense of duty by refusing to leave the beach under duress. He climbed into the pinnace. Edgar managed to scramble onto some nearby rocks which left him up to the knees in water, and, somewhat precariously balanced, he dodged what stones he could. A Hawaiian seized hold of a broken oar left on the beach by the pinnace's crew and waded out to strike Edgar with it. Seeing this, Vancouver jumped out of the pinnace and grabbed at the man, getting hit by the oar for his pains. Another Hawaiian joined in the assault and beat at Edgar with a flat piece of board until it split in two. The assault was becoming a serious affair, certainly the most violent of any to date. Fortunately, Parea stepped into the fray and ordered the Hawaiians to desist, which they did immediately. He told Edgar and Vancouver that their best interest would be served if they took the pinnace and went back to the ship. However, this was impossible, given the state of the pinnace; all the oars had been stolen in the mêlée and anything else that could be removed had also gone.

Parea agreed to get the oars returned, and left the scene with the ostensible intention of doing so, but his departure released the crowd from restraint. The Hawaiians began collecting stones and the situation was back to where it was before Parea had intervened. Edgar decided that if he could not quit the beach by sea he would quit it by going inland to look for Captain Cook. This was an extraordinary decision, for it meant going through the hostile crowd. Not surprisingly, Vancouver decided not to go with him. But this left Vancouver alone on the beach by the pinnace. As soon as Edgar left the beach the Hawaiians attacked triumphantly, as they were assured of success against one unarmed young boy. They pushed Vancouver aside, knocked him down and continued to ransack the boat. They were trying to knock the ring bolts out of the stem and stern of the boat when Edgar returned. He had scrambled over some rocks to try to avoid the crowd but had been intercepted by three Hawaiians who 'persuaded' him to accompany them to Parea. When they found Parea he had with him a Hawaiian who was carrying two oars, one of them broken, and together they returned to the beach.

Again, Parea told them to leave the beach for their own safety, and to this end they called in the cutter, which had been lying off out of range of the stones, and departed for the *Discovery*, towing the pinnace behind them. On the way they went to the shore camp at the nearby village of Kakooa to report to Captain Cook when he returned from his wild goose chase in the neighbouring area. The pinnace's crew had a lot of explaining to do. After all, they had abandoned the captain's boat, and it was not in a fit condition to take him back to the *Resolution* with the dignity necessary for a commander-in-chief. Edgar, as the senior man in the rather bruised and dispirited group, had to make the report, and Cook was furious about what had happened. Not only had he been made to look foolish by the Hawaiians, who had led him a merry dance in the hinterland, but his own boat was wrecked and the Hawaiians had engaged with impunity in a violent assault on his men. Thus, the important chance to make a show of strength, and give an example of the kind of punishment at his disposal, had been lost: if the Hawaiians could get away with this assault, they would only increase their depredations the next time. Captain Cook told Lieutenant King that, to his 'sorrow', 'the behaviour of the Indians would at last oblige him to use force; for that they must not he said imagine they have gained an advantage over us' (King's ms. Log and Proceedings). Cook also copied Clerke's decision to clear the ship of visitors, and to this effect all women and ordinary Hawaiians were turned out of the *Resolution* immediately he got back on board.

But what of Parea? He knew that his 'victory' in the affray on the beach would not be ignored by Captain Cook. He did not know, of course, what Captain Cook would do, and to this end he had tried to sound out the likely reaction immediately after the two boats left the cove. He jumped into a canoe and came after Edgar, and as a peace offering returned Vancouver's midshipman's cap. According to Edgar's Log, he asked Edgar 'if he should come on board in the morning whether we should not hurt him for what had happened, we answered in the Negative'. With this intelligence, Parea departed across the bay to the other village of Kowrowa where Terreeoboo was living. Edgar presumably blamed himself for what had happened, and this was the reason for his magnanimity towards Parea.

Cook knew that the result of the affray was a bad blow to his standing with the Hawaiians, and that as news of the rout of the boat crews spread, with apparently no response from the visitors, relations would deteriorate unless he could restore the situation quickly. The trouble-seeking party among the Hawaiians had gained an advantage over Cook. No amount of excuses could rationalise that away. King was told by Cook to return to the *Discovery*, interview Edgar again and get a detailed account of what had happened. At the next morning's conference King was to report on the affray and Cook would then decide what measures to take, if any. Unfortunately, before Lieutenant King's report could be given, a far more serious incident took place which forced Cook into the hasty action that cost him his life.

IV

Theft of the Cutter

The affray on the beach left everybody on edge. Cook's request for fuller details of what happened is one indication of the dissatisfaction he felt about the outcome of the affair. He had already received a verbal report at the observatory and it is not clear exactly what additional information Lieutenant King was expected to glean from Edgar and Vancouver. Cook's unease passed on to King, who was perhaps also influenced by his interviews on the *Discovery* with Edgar, Vancouver and others. King slept at the shore-camp, as officer in charge of the observatory and the *Resolution*'s mast, and he gave new orders to the doubled guard of marines who were to keep watch during the night. They were told to be specially vigilant for Hawaiian intruders, and if any came near the morai bent on mischief they were to be fired at. This was a direct and specific instruction and clearly shows Captain Cook's determination to impose a tougher policy for dealing with those Hawaiians who misbehaved or threatened mischief towards the ships, their property or the people belonging to them.

During the night, after eleven o'clock, several Hawaiians approached the shore-camp and a sentry fired at one of them near midnight. He missed his man but scared off further intruders. His vigilance directed the attentions of the Hawaiians who were bent on trouble towards softer targets. Unable to sneak into the shore-camp because of the armed and determined guards, some Hawaiians turned their minds to a completely unprotected prize. This was the *Discovery*'s launch, which was moored to one of the anchor buoys and sunk below the water level to protect it from the fierce heat of the day. It was an easy target for a people well versed in manipulating wooden objects through the surf. They were so silent and unobtrusive about their work that they managed to cut through the moorings, raise the boat and carry it away without anybody on the *Discovery* or on shore hearing a thing. The boat was broken up within a few hours of being stolen and was not recovered.

The *Discovery*'s large cutter was the biggest boat it had and extremely valuable. On this voyage each ship had two cutters, a large one and a small one. They were short, broad working boats used to convey stores. The other boats carried were the *Resolution*'s launch, the biggest boat of all, which could take up to two dozen men and a quantity of stores; the *Discovery*'s launch; the captain's pinnace, which had a crew of eight and was generally used by the captain and officers for journeys between the ships and the shore; and each ship's jolly-boat, a light message boat used by midshipmen on their errands. This was by far the most serious theft on the Third Voyage so far, and meant inestimable damage to the expedition, because of the heavy reliance placed on the ships' boats in near-shore work, and in manoeuvring among ice-packs in northern waters. Loss of a boat could seriously hamper the effectiveness of the expedition when they returned for another look for a northern passage above the Bering Straits.

The larger cutter contained a lot of iron, and this alone may have been sufficient inducement to steal the boat. Cook once remarked when discussing the Polynesian proclivity to theft of iron: 'An Indian among penny knives and beads, and even nails and broken glass, is in the same state of mind as the meanest servant in Europe among unlocked coffers of jewels and gold' (quoted in Barrow, 1835, p.19). The Hawaiians may also have had another motive. Samwell refers to this in his account of the incident. He wrote: 'To widen the Breach between us, the Indians, last Night, took away our large Cutter' (Samwell, ms. Journal). The implication is that the theft was deliberately intended to be provocative by a party among the Hawaiians. Parea was blamed by several Hawaiians as the author of the theft. He is alleged to have put his men up to it, either for the iron in the cutter, or, more likely, to make trouble. Or he might have been smarting still over the affray with Edgar; after all, though his side won the contest, he had been struck over the head with an oar. There are a few points in the story which suggest his innocence. He was last seen paddling away to Kowrowa on the side of the bay furthest from the *Discovery*. Why, therefore, if he was guilty, did his men not steal a boat from the *Resolution*? This ship was moored closer to Kowrowa than the *Discovery*. All things being equal it should have presented a more tempting target. Things may not have been equal, however. Cook's men may have been more vigilant than Clerke's, and Parea's anger might have been directed more towards Clerke and the *Discovery* than Cook and the *Resolution* because it was with Edgar of the *Discovery* that he had quarrelled (though it was a seaman from the *Resolution*'s pinnace who had struck him with the oar). Parea does not appear to have been seen by anybody the next day; this is not necessarily guilty behaviour. He may merely have been over-anxious about his possible reception by Cook because of the affray with Edgar, and he could have taken himself and his party inland to let matters cool down. It is possible that Parea had nothing to do with the boat theft at all, and perhaps, for that matter, nothing to do with the theft of the tongs in the first place (Beaglehole, 1974, p.666; his assessment of Parea is that he 'seems to have been an admirable man', p.665). He may have been blamed afterwards by the ship's officers on entirely circumstantial grounds and the accusations of Hawaiians.

The exact timing of events on the morning of 14 February is not easy to untangle. Different accounts give different times for the same events, disagreeing by as much as an hour or even two hours. I assume that the loss of the cutter would have been discovered at first light, approximately 6.15 a.m. at that time of year. The cutter was found to be missing by Lieutenant Burney, who had the watch on the *Discovery* (Clerke, ms. Journal). The matter was clearly out of Clerke's hands, given the magnitude of the loss, and he needed advice on what to do about attempting to recover the boat. The first thing he ordered was a check on the moorings that had held the cutter to the small bower anchor buoy (Clerke, ms. Journal; Burney, 1779). A boat was sent to the buoy and on its return the officer reported that the four-inch rope had been cut through 'by some instrument or other' (Clerke, ms. Journal). The missing boat had clearly been stolen.

Captain Clerke took a boat across to the *Resolution* to inform Captain Cook what had happened during the night. The Captains consulted each other about what to do. Cook had certainly been presented with the desired opportunity to force a showdown with the trouble-makers, but the main problem was to identify the culprits. The boat and the thieves had disappeared. Cook's reaction was to make plans to seize the canoes present in the bay and hold them for ransom against the return of the *Discovery*'s cutter. At first this seemed an excellent idea. These canoes were valuable objects among the

Hawaiians. Their loss would deal a crippling blow to the local economy and social life. The night before, Parea had violently objected to Edgar's attempt to seize one of his personal canoes, and the other chiefs in the bay at that time could be expected to be equally determined to secure the safe custody of their own canoes if they were threatened. Given a little time there was no doubt that the boat, if it was still in one piece (which we know now it was not), would have been returned to secure the release of the canoes. Thus far Cook's behaviour was restrained and, in the light of the seriousness of the theft, it was also equitable – Hawaiian canoes for the British boat.

According to Captain Clerke, they discussed the theft and the measures to be taken, and then Captain Cook issued him with orders. Clerke is specific that Cook's plan at this moment was confined to a seizure of the canoes. Nothing was said to him by Captain Cook about any further measures. This information is important because it separates the action taken to seal off the bay from the subsequent action taken to seize King Terreeoboo. It conflicts with other reports, notably Lieutenant King's official account, which states that Cook's plan from the start was to seize the King, and that his reserve plan, if he failed to catch King Terreeoboo, was to seize the canoes. I think the evidence makes better sense if Clerke's version is followed, and one assumes that Captain Cook changed his plan. The arguments for and against this view will be discussed in the next chapter; first, I will look at the preparations made to seal off the bay, and also describe the layout of the bay itself. The last is essential for a full understanding of what happened in the next few hours.

Bligh's sketch of Kealakekua Bay shows the positions that morning of the ships, *Resolution* and *Discovery*, relative to the main features of the bay. The *Resolution* was anchored about a quarter of a mile from the *Discovery*. The distance across the bay from the north-west point to the south-east point is just over a mile and a quarter (on Bligh's sketch). It is not a large bay but it is fairly deep. The bottom drops away rapidly from the black volcanic sand beaches. The main feature of the shore-line is the sharply rising cliff that separates the points. This cliff face rises from the north-west point where Kowrowa village was situated, and continues to rise throughout its length until it towers several hundred feet above the site of the old village of Kakooa. It is impassable along the shore except at very low tide, and to travel from Kowrowa to Kakooa by land would involve a fairly stiff climb up the steep slopes of the hillside behind Kowrowa, and another climb over the length of the cliff face before dropping down the steeper sides of the hill beyond Kakooa. The distance involved, because of the extreme height of the high land, would be more than double the direct distance between the villages by canoe. The hillside immediately above the open rock of the cliff is almost vertical and correspondingly difficult and dangerous to traverse. The only safe way is to cross much further up the hill where the slope is relatively, but not much, flatter.

The steepness and inaccessibility of the cliff face made it an ideal place for refuge. Persons and goods could be lowered on ropes to the many open caves that dotted its face. There was no way to climb up to these caves from the sea, and an attempt to gain entry by lowering oneself down the face was impractical if the person in the cave was determined to resist entry. For this reason the Hawaiians used the caves to hide people, such as Terreeoboo, if they were threatened. After Cook's death there are reports that the Hawaiians were seen, through the ships' telescopes, doing just this with their King to prevent any attempt by Cook's men to arrest or harm him in revenge for what had happened to Cook.

The two villages at each end of the cliff were in contact by canoe and the distance across the bay could be covered in a matter of minutes. The majority of the Hawaiians who came to see Cook made their temporary residence at Kowrowa in quickly assembled grass-covered huts which reminded the British visitors of haystacks.[1] The priests resided at Kakooa, close against the hillside and by the fresh water spring (the nearby pond tended to be brackish). There were many Hawaiians, however, living in huts near Kakooa and spread out along and beyond the southern point. The visitors remarked that there were many tidy and well-laid-out plantations in the area and that it appeared to be a pleasant enough place to reside in. The priestly settlement and the morai at Kakooa gave a semblance of permanency to Kealakekua.

With the two ships anchored approximately in the middle of the bay, any intending escapers would need to paddle out into the sea between one of the ships and the shore. The foul ground near the shore was less of a problem for the Hawaiian canoes than the ships'

---

[1] They did strikingly resemble haystacks, as can be seen from the life-size model hut in the Bernice P. Bishop Museum, Honolulu.

boats, but what the boats lacked in shallowness of draught they could make up for with their muskets: even if they could not follow a canoe close to the rocks, they could deter it from escaping by firing at it. Cook's plan was to place the ships' boats between the points of the bay to act as chasers if any Hawaiian canoe made a break for it.

Cook gave specific orders that the boats were to be 'well manned and armed' (Clerke, ms. Journal). One can infer from what happened later that he ordered the use of ball shot and not of small shot only; ball shot could kill, while small shot would only pepper and sting. Small shot was only effective at point-blank range. Clerke does not mention the type of shot ordered, but when King arrived on board the *Resolution* to collect the time-keeper later that morning he found 'the marines arming and Captain Cook loading his double barrelled gun'. From the evidence of the firing that took place later we know that Captain Cook loaded his double piece with small shot in one barrel and ball shot in the other. The marines whom King found arming all had ball in their muskets when they were called upon to fire on the beach. The crew of the pinnace under Henry Roberts also fired ball later, in the fight on the beach; accounts describe their effect on the Hawaiians in phrases such as 'great execution' (Harvey, ms. Log), 'much execution' (Law, ms. Journal), 'keeping up a very hot fire' (Ledyard, in Sparks, 1828), 'many of them dropped' (Samwell, ms. Journal) and 'under cover of a smart fire' (King, 1784). Williamson's launch and Lanyon's small cutter, which were sent to the north point before Cook left the *Resolution*, were both armed with muskets and ball shot. Certainly when Lanyon's crew fired into the remaining Hawaiians near Captain Cook's body they fired with ball, because they killed one of them. This is consistent with Cook's orders to Lieutenant King the day before (King, 1784): Cook 'ordered me, in case of their beginning to throw stones, or behave insolently, immediately to fire a ball at the offenders. I accordingly gave orders to the corporal, to have the pieces of the sentinels loaded with ball, instead of small shot.'

Cook gave orders to Clerke to send two boats from the *Discovery* to the south-eastern point to 'prevent any Canoes going away and if any attempted it to drive them onshore' (Clerke, ms. Journal). Clerke does not mention any orders for the men to fire their muskets, but other accounts are specific that Cook did order them to fire if necessary (e.g. Samwell, ms. Journal and 1786, p.12). If Lieutenant King's report is correct (1784), some of the great guns of one of the ships, presumably the *Discovery*, were at some time fired at two canoes attempting to run the gauntlet. To fire ship's guns involved preparation and direct command from the Captain; if any were fired at this time (before Cook left for the shore) then Cook either ordered it himself or had included this in his orders to Clerke.

Clerke went back to the *Discovery* and ordered the Second Lieutenant, John Rickman, to take 'the Launch and the small Cutter with their Crews and some Marines well arm'd to the station Capt Cook had assign'd them' (Clerke, ms. Journal). Other accounts agree with Clerke in clearly stating that the two boats at the southern point were the *Discovery*'s launch and cutter (Law's ms. Journal, Burney's ms. Journal, Samwell's ms. Journal); but confusion has been caused on this point by William Bayly, the *Discovery*'s Astronomer, who stated in his ms. Log and Journal that Cook 'ordered the *Discovery*'s launch and his own great cutter to the East side of the Bay ... Mr Rickman commanded the *Discovery*'s launch and Mr Blythe [Bligh] commanded the cutter.' This is most unlikely; if Bligh in the *Resolution*'s large cutter had gone to the southern point with the *Discovery*'s launch to form the guarding party, this would have left Clerke's small cutter free, and Clerke would have used that boat, not his jolly-boat, when he returned to the *Resolution*. But he clearly says 'I soon after took the Jolly Boat (which now was the only boat I had left) and came to the *Resolution*'. And he later mentions musket fire at the point as coming from 'my Launch and small Cutter'. Bayly was on shore at the observatory, and was probably confusing the initial orders with what happened soon afterwards. Some later accounts believe Bayly's unique statement, for instance Hough (1972, p.43); Hough uses Bayly to suit his case against Bligh.

While Clerke was carrying out his orders, Cook also sent two of his boats to the north-western point under the command of the Third Lieutenant, John Williamson, to carry out the same instructions. Williamson took the *Resolution*'s launch and small cutter to his station, his men armed and ready for action. In the small cutter he had a party of five midshipmen. From the account of an anonymous officer on the *Resolution*, it appears that Clerke did not get his boats to their positions until the time when Cook left his ship to go ashore. While the boats were taking up their positions, a large ocean canoe was spotted under sail in the bay and making for the open sea. If Clerke was not yet ready with his boats something had to be done quickly to catch the canoe before it got out to sea. Cook had his pinnace and the *Resolution*'s large cutter available. The cutter was already manned and armed. He ordered his Master, William Bligh, to take the cutter and get after the canoe.[2] This Bligh quickly did and was soon close enough to the canoe to signal its occupants to heave-to. Apparently verbal persuasion was not enough, and Bligh ordered his men to fire at the canoe, which forced it to veer away from its seaward course and head straight for the beach at the southern end of the bay. The occupants landed and ran inland, abandoning their canoe on some rocks.

The timing of this chase by Bligh is important, because it establishes that Cook's orders were to fire on canoes attempting to escape. Bligh was sent on this mission by Cook personally before he left the *Resolution*. Nobody who knows anything about Bligh's attitude to orders from superiors would doubt for a moment that if he opened fire on a canoe in these circumstances it was because he had been told to do so by Captain Cook. But Bligh's obedience to his orders may have made the consequences of those orders clearer to Cook, as we shall see in the next chapter.

---

[2] In sending Bligh on this mission, Cook unwittingly deprived himself of the services of the only reliable armed boat party at his disposal. Judging by Bligh's actions on other occasions, he would certainly have tried to land when violence erupted, and might have succeeded in taking off Cook and the marines without loss of life. See p.89 for Bligh's defence of the morai; and Kennedy (1978, pp. 115-16) for his successful evacuation of the beach at Tofoa in 1789.

V

A Change of Plan

Did Captain Cook decide to seize a hostage from the start of the morning's deliberations, or did he change his mind under the pressure of events? Lieutenant King stated that the former was the case (King, 1784), and most accounts have followed him. Many books on Cook simply lifted King's narrative, not always acknowledging their source. But this version leaves contradictions which only an acceptance of the second proposition can make consistent.

Captain Clerke recorded in his ms. Journal, which appears from internal evidence to have been written the same day, that he discussed the incident of the stolen cutter with Captain Cook and that the decision was made to seal off the bay and prevent canoes escaping. When Clerke returned to the *Discovery* and issued orders to his boats, he decided, for some reason which is not recorded, that he needed to discuss the matter further with Cook. He writes: 'I soon after took the Jolly Boat (which now was the only Boat I had left) and came to the *Resolution* with an intention of having some more discourse with Capt Cook upon this business.' But before he got back to the *Resolution* Lieutenant Gore hailed him as he approached in the jolly-boat and told him that Captain Cook had gone ashore to see Terreeoboo. Clerke continues:

Lt Gore told me that Captain Cook was gone with his Pinnace, Launch and small Cutter to a Town situated just within the NW Point, where King Terre'aboo and the major part of the People of consequence then resided, upon which I return'd to my Ship, concluding as Capt Cook was gone to the King, matters would soon be settled, for we were as yet by no means upon bad terms with Arees [warriors] or any body else. There were at this time many small Canoes trading about the Ships.

As far as Clerke was concerned, Cook's visit to Terreeoboo was an initiative that would settle the problem; once the King intervened the thieves would be forced to give up the boat. This account has a ring of truth in it. Clerke had no axe to grind about his role. He suggests that he was not implicated in the preparations to arrest Terreeoboo and he betrays not the slightest knowledge that the King was to be molested in any way. He assumed that Cook was going to see the King to reason with him and get his support, and the trump card Cook held was the threat to the Hawaiian canoes which were trapped in the bay by the ship's boats. The idea that Cook was attempting to seize the Hawaiian King did not, I think, occur to Clerke even when he was told that Cook had gone ashore with an armed party.

On his return to the *Discovery*, Clerke sent his one remaining boat, the little jolly-boat, to Lieutenant Rickman at the southern point, with orders for him to use it to tow back to the ship any canoes he impounded while on patrol: '... soon after I got onboard I observ'd some Muskets discharg'd from my Launch and small Cutter upon which I sent the Jolly Boat to know how matters went, and Orders to Lieut Rickman if he made any seizures of Canoes to send them to the Ship by the Jolly Boat.' In other words, as far as Clerke was concerned the original plan was still operating, and Captain Cook's visit to Terreeoboo was simply to inform him of the seizure of the canoes. Clerke's job was still to continue to blockade the canoes and seize any which attempted to escape. Clerke would surely not have sent away his one remaining boat, thus stranding him on the *Discovery* and making physical communication either with the shore or the *Resolution* impossible, if he had believed Cook intended anything as dangerous as arresting King Terreeoboo on a crowded and hostile shore. Clerke's account is consistent with the suggestion that it was after his interview with Clerke that Cook decided to intensify his measures from impounding the Hawaiian canoes to arresting King Terreeoboo; or at least that Cook did not disclose to Clerke the full extent of the measures he was about to take.

A complication is introduced here by Lieutenant Burney, who asserted many years after the voyage that Cook ordered Clerke to go ashore and bring the King back with him, but because of his ill-health Clerke had to beg leave to be excused, so that Cook was compelled to go ashore himself (Burney, 1819, p.260). Corporal Ledyard of the *Resolution*, in his book published in 1783, had made much the same allegation (p.143). In his Journal, written at the time of the incident, Burney made no reference to Clerke's excusing himself from Cook's plan to arrest the King. His book was not published until forty years after Kealakekua Bay, and he may have been jogging his memory with the help of Ledyard's book. He was pointedly not following King's official version of 1784. Burney was unlikely to have been present with Cook and Clerke that morning (unless he accompanied Clerke to give a report on his watch), and he may have assumed that Ledyard, who was almost certainly attached to the shore camp (King, 1784, refers to orders he gave to the Corporal), had witnessed the conversation as he reported it. There seems little reason for Clerke to have omitted this incident in his own account, if it had happened: ill-health is not a dishonourable reason for failing duty.

King also refers to the matter in his ms. Log: 'Captn Clerke had been on board to acquaint C Cook of the loss of his boat, but was too unwell to go ashore to Terreeoboo to enquire after it & to get him on board. C Cook therefore himself went ...' (ms. Log and Proceedings). But King left it out of the published version of 1784. He was not present when Cook and Clerke spoke together and may have inferred it from something Cook said; perhaps he asked Cook why Clerke did not go ashore to get his own boat back, and Cook replied that Clerke was too ill. Cook's statement of fact about the general state of Clerke's health may have been transformed into a report that Clerke appealed for an excusal of duty on grounds of his health. The fact that King and Ledyard were of this opinion in their Logs, but Clerke and Burney were not, is telling evidence that something like this happened, further endorsed by King's dropping the incident when he came to write up the official version. King had access to Clerke's Log after his death as official author, and he would have noted how Clerke explains the morning's events. Corporal Ledyard, who either got the story from King at the shore camp or was present with King during the interview with Cook, had no reason to revise his account. Burney simply followed Ledyard – after all, the story was plausible once the authors lost sight of the fact that Cook's plans were not premeditated but were changed without notice in the rush of events.

The disposition of the boats in the bay is another piece of evidence for the view that Cook changed his mind. He had ordered Clerke to send two boats, well manned and armed, to the southern point and he himself sent two boats to the northern point under the command of Williamson. These boats were in position in a rough line across the bay that passed behind the ships on the seaward side. It was only as Cook

rowed past the northern point on his way to Kowrowa that he called
upon Williamson.to leave his station and join him. Cook thereby
altered an earlier instruction belonging to the earlier plan. His choice of
Williamson was unfortunate, but that he altered a previous plan is
beyond doubt.

If Cook changed his mind, what induced him to do so? The answer
lies in both what had been happening in the previous twenty hours,
which had made him determined to disabuse the Hawaiians of the
illusion that they had got the better of him, and what was now
happening in the bay. Kealakekua Bay is small, and the steep slopes
behind the bay would amplify the sound of gunfire. While Cook and
Clerke were organising the disposition of their boats across the bay,
the *Resolution*'s large cutter commanded by Bligh had, as we saw, been
ordered to chase a large canoe ashore. This canoe was chased with
gunfire to the southern shore, and King reports that some of the big
guns were later fired at two other canoes: 'Whilst I was on board some
Great Guns were fyrd at large canoes which were rowing off; in order
to make them return on shore' (ms. Log and Proceedings). The noise
in the bay must have been substantial. Some of the Hawaiians would
not have known what was going on, but it was certainly not usual for
the visitors to wake the entire populace with so much noise. Of course,
many of the Hawaiians were not entirely bereft of ideas as to what
might have provoked the noise from the visitors. Some of them had
participated in the theft of the cutter, and many others by that
morning knew about the theft. They would be expecting something to
happen. If 'noisy sticks' were used when a simple item of iron was
captured it followed that even noisier sticks would be used when a large
prize such as the boat was removed.

Captain Cook, watching on the *Resolution* and hearing the heavy
echoes of the musket and gunfire in the bay, would have realised that
unless something was done quickly the King and his entourage,
fearing for their safety, would probably melt away into the land
behind the bay. Once the bay was deserted, the sanction of seizing the
canoes would not result in the return of the cutter; there would be
nobody of importance to threaten or to bargain with. Cook was in no
mood for half measures nor was he the most patient of men.
Lieutenant King included in his published assessment of Captain
Cook's character (1784) that 'His temper might perhaps have been
justly blamed, as subject to hastiness and passion'. At this moment

A

VOYAGE

TO THE

PACIFIC OCEAN.

UNDERTAKEN,

BY THE COMMAND OF HIS MAJESTY,

FOR MAKING

Difcoveries in the Northern Hemifphere.

TO DETERMINE

The POSITION and EXTENT of the WEST SIDE of NORTH AMERICA;
its DISTANCE from ASIA; and the PRACTICABILITY of a
NORTHERN PASSAGE to EUROPE.

PERFORMED UNDER THE DIRECTION OF

Captains COOK, CLERKE, and GORE,

In his MAJESTY's Ships the RESOLUTION and DISCOVERY.
In the Years 1776, 1777, 1778, 1779, and 1780.

IN THREE VOLUMES.

VOL. I. and II. written by Captain JAMES COOK, F.R.S.
VOL. III. by Captain JAMES KING, LL.D. and F.R.S.

Illuftrated with MAPS and CHARTS, from the Original Drawings made by Lieut. HENRY ROBERTS,
under the Direction of Captain COOK; and with a great Variety of Portraits of Perfons, Views
of Places, and Hiftorical Reprefentations of Remarkable Incidents, drawn by Mr.
WEBBER during the Voyage, and engraved by the moft eminent Artifts.

Publifhed by Order of the Lords Commiffioners of the Admiralty.

VOL. III.

LONDON:

PRINTED BY W. AND A. STRAHAN:
FOR G. NICOL, BOOKSELLER TO HIS MAJESTY, IN THE STRAND;
AND T. CADELL, IN THE STRAND.
MDCCLXXXIV.

1. The title page of Vol. III of the official account of Captain Cook's last voyage, written by James King, and published in 1784. Note that the maps and charts, many of them by Bligh, are all attributed to Lieut. Henry Roberts.

2. The Cook Memorial Medal struck by the Royal Society to commemorate him after his death.

3. Portrait of Captain James King from the frontispiece of Vol. III of the official account. Painted by Samuel Shelley and engraved by L. Hogg.

4. 'Terreoboo, king of Owyhee, bringing presents to Captain Cook', from Cook and King, 1784. From a drawing by John Webber, who was draftsman on the voyage.

5. 'A view of Karakakooa in Owyhee', from Cook and King, 1784. From a drawing by Webber.

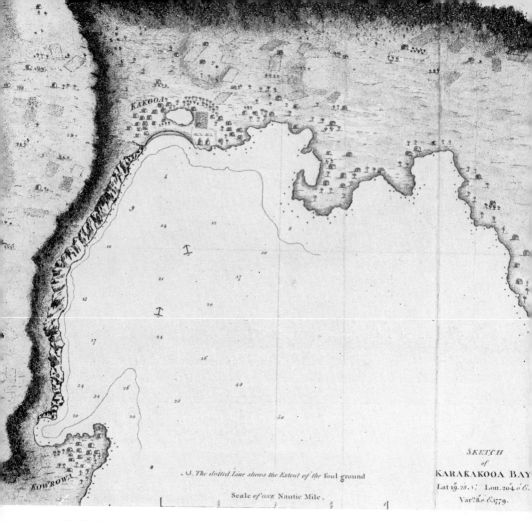

6. Bligh's chart of Kealakakua Bay, from Cook and King, 1784. North is towards the left side of the map.

7. A portable observatory of the type used on Cook's last voyage. Designed by William Bayly (1776).

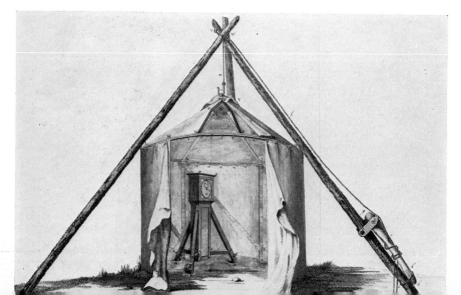

8. 'An offering before Captain Cook, in the Sandwich Islands', from Cook and King, 1784. Engraved by S. Middiman and J. Hall. From a drawing by Webber.

9. 'A morai in Atoot', from Cook and King, 1784. From a drawing by Webber.

10. The death of Captain Cook, by John Webber. Engraved by F. Bartolozzi and W. Byrne. Engravings of this picture were published in 1784. Webber decided to follow the official line, that when he was killed Cook was

11. The death of Captain Cook, by George Carter. First exhibited in London in 1785. Carter appears to have been following the accounts of Edgar and Law, whose journals remained unpublished until 1928 (see Gould, 1928a), rather than the official account by Captain King. Engraved by S. Smith, I. Hall and I. Thornthwaite.

12. The death of Captain Cook, by Johann Zoffany. Undated (C. Mitchell in *Burlington Magazine*, 1944, p. 56, estimates the date to be between 1789 and 1797). Zoffany opted out of the controversy and simply depicts Cook dying. His depiction of Lieut. Phillips is influenced by Webber.

13. The death of Captain Cook, a coloured aquatint by Francis Jukes after a picture by John Clevely, based on a drawing by James Clevely, his brother, who was a carpenter on the *Resolution*. The aquatint was published in 1788. Clevely follows the Webber line.

both natural inclination and the needs of the immediate situation coincided. Action had to be taken if the object of his efforts was not to slip away. If they got away with this particular theft there would be no respect left. Without respect on both sides there was bound to be serious trouble.

I think it was probably at some time between the departure of Bligh in the *Resolution*'s large cutter to chase the canoe and the arrival on board of Lieutenant King that Cook decided to go ashore. Lieutenant King arrived just before seven o'clock on the *Resolution* from the shore camp, where he had spent the night. He came to report to Captain Cook about the incidents around the observatory between eleven and midnight during the night before, and to report on what he had been told by Edgar and Vancouver. He also had a regular duty to carry out, namely to collect the ship's valuable time-keeper and take it ashore for the observatory's use during the day's astronomical work. King describes (ms. Log and Proceedings) the scene he found on the Resolution: 'On board the Resolution I found them all arming themselves, & the Captn loading his double Barreld piece; on my going to acquaint him with the nights adventure, he interrupted me & said we are not arming for the last nights affair, they have Stolen the Discoverys Cutter, & it is for that we are making preparation.' If Cook's mind was almost made up about what he intended to do, King's account of the night before did nothing to calm him down. Edgar and Vancouver's experiences, shots in the night, and now the cutter! The Hawaiians were due a lesson in relative superiority. To contemplate going ashore with an armed guard was a new experience for Cook in Hawaii. To underline his determination he loaded his double-barrelled gun, one barrel with small shot and one with ball shot, i.e., one to frighten the ignorant and one to kill the insolent. If the Hawaiians remained ignorant then small shot would do, but if he thought they were trifling with him, then Cook would kill one of them as an example of his power. There can be no other interpretation of his actions in loading the gun in that way.

We can still, however, detect elements of lack of thought and inadequate preparation. Cook was going ashore with a small party of men and only one barrel of his gun loaded with lethal shot. His other officers were deployed on the ships or in the boats. He was completely confident that he would prevail, but he neglected to consider the seriousness of the steps he was about to take. His small force of marines was armed with ball, but there were only nine of them altogether and they were not very well-trained. To support them, he armed the seamen in the pinnace under the command of a Master's Mate, Henry Roberts. Again this was not enough for him, and as he moved towards the village he called over Lieutenant Williamson's launch with its armed seamen to support his party. This left the small cutter at the point to continue the blockade duty under the command of Master's Mate Lanyon. Thus, as the implications of his action took clearer shape, Cook added more force to his party. If he had contemplated calmly the seriousness of what he was attempting he would have taken a party of at least sixty armed marines and seamen with him. But this option was precluded by his earlier decision to close the bay, because the men necessary for that task were scattered in boats up to a mile or so away from the *Resolution*. He could not get the boats recalled quickly and time was of the essence at this moment. To delay while drawing the force together would have given Terreeoboo a chance to escape inland.

Stopping Terreeoboo escaping was his main task once the gunfire had sounded the alarm in the bay. It was a short step from the idea of stopping the king escaping to deciding to incarcerate him on the ship. We cannot be sure when Cook took this step mentally, but I think it was probably quite late in the enterprise, after he had spoken to Lieutenant King. The taking of hostages was not new to Cook. He had done this several times in the Pacific before and it had generally brought a successful conclusion to arguments about thefts. King inserted a statement to this effect in his published account (but not in his Log) between his description of Cook's activity on the *Resolution*, when he was interrupted by Cook while giving his reports, and his being told by Cook that he was going ashore. 'It had been his usual practice,' writes King, 'whenever any thing of consequence was lost, at any of the islands in this ocean, to get the king or some of the principal Erees, on board, and keep them as hostages, till it was restored. This method, which had been always attended with success, he meant to pursue on the present occasion' (King 1784). In this way King created the impression that Cook had determined to try the hostage policy from the start. This was the implication that readers took from his book. King ignores the fact that Cook's behaviour on this Third Voyage was more aggressive and punitive than on previous voyages. The taking of hostages in the past had almost been a gentlemanly affair, with the chiefs concerned invariably co-operating. At Tahiti on this voyage Cook had gone much further to recover stolen property than he had ever done on the First and Second Voyages: he had seized canoes and burnt them or broken them up. He had also marched across the countryside burning and destroying Tahitian houses and other property until the object that had been stolen – a goat – was returned. Thus taking Terreeoboo hostage with an armed party of marines was far more aggressive than the acts King mentions, but consistent with the picture of Cook as a tired and impatient man on this, his last voyage (Beaglehole, 1974, pp. 558-9).

King goes on, in the passage quoted above from the 1784 account, to change the order of events regarding the activity already under way in the bay. He writes: '... and *at the same time*, [Cook] had given orders to stop all the canoes that should attempt to leave the bay, with an intention of seizing and destroying them, if he could not recover the cutter by peaceable means' (my italics). But Cook's plan as presented by King was hopeless, indeed senseless. Seizing the canoes, according to King, was a last resort if 'peaceable' means failed; but if the arrest of the King and his principal chiefs was to be peaceable, why take armed men ashore to accomplish it? More, if taking the King hostage was insufficient to achieve the return of the boat – a most unlikely event given the veneration for the Hawaiian King among his subjects – why would the subsequent burning of the canoes succeed in forcing the Hawaiians to comply? If it was Cook's first intention to seize the King as hostage, his secondary plan completely negated his first objective. Seizing the King required some element of surprise; they would have to persuade him to go on board the *Resolution* without creating fears in him or his subjects that he was threatened. But this was made impossible by the blockade of the canoes, which inevitably meant gunfire and thus a warning for the Hawaiians. If surprise was impossible, many more armed men were needed, but having dispersed the boats across the bay Cook had dispersed the very armed force he needed to overcome resistance. The two plans cannot be welded into one sensible strategy.

Lieutenant King and Captain Cook left the *Resolution* together 'between seven and eight o'clock' (King, 1784). King took his boat back to Kakooa, carrying with him the time-keeper. Captain Cook stepped into his pinnace and headed for Kowrowa. A glimpse of Cook's mood at this time is preserved in an anonymous diary kept by one of the officers of the *Resolution* which records an exchange between himself and Captain Cook. Just as Cook was leaving his ship he noted the progress that Bligh had made in his chase of the Hawaiian canoe. Bligh had chased the canoe onto the shore at the southern end of the bay. The Hawaiians had abandoned their canoe and left it lodged on the rocks. Bligh, however, was unable to get close in because of the foul ground just below water level which threatened his boat. The officer writes: 'I was then standing by Captain Cook when he said that canoe was in our possession, and that a boat might bring it on board if it was wanted I replyed to him that if the people came in such numbers as they did the evening before it would hardly be possible, if they have one musket (or words to the same effect) says he its enough I am sure they will not stand the fire of a musket' (anon., 1779b). The reference to the evening before is to the incident between Edgar and Parea. Burney's Journal (quoted in Manwaring, 1931, p.133) refers to this conversation: 'Captain Cook, who was then leaving the ship, was very positive the Indians would not stand the fire of a single musket: indeed, so many instances had occurred which all helped confirm his opinion.' In his ms. Journal Burney has added 'that it is not to be wondered at, if everybody thought the same'. Burney was serving in the *Discovery* that morning and could not have heard the conversation; he must have been told of it in the exchange of information that occurred after Cook's death.

This short remark gives us a clear illustration of Cook's mood at this point. He had armed the boat parties so that if resisted they should use their weapons. He was determined on a show-down, and if this somehow escaped Clerke and King, it did not escape Bligh. Cook looked with approval on Bligh's work against the canoe, and was intent on emulating the hard line himself when he got ashore. And he still had that fatal confidence in the efficiency of a few musket-shots against any amount of Hawaiians.

Cook's shore party consisted of himself, Lieutenant Molesworth Phillips of the marines, Sergeant Gibson, Corporal Thomas and seven private marines; his support was made up of Master's Mate Henry Roberts, the crew of the pinnace (probably about ten seamen, all armed), and Lieutenant Williamson and his boat-party (about a dozen seamen, all armed). A short distance away, at the point, the small cutter was under the command of Master's Mate Lanyon with four midshipmen, Ward, Taylor, Charlton and Trevenen, and several seamen. They too were armed. The pinnace went to the rocky shore-line by the village of Kowrowa, where Cook and the marines disembarked and formed up to march into the village. Roberts was ordered to take the pinnace away from the rocks and ride on oars and Williamson was ordered to do likewise a few yards from the pinnace. Both boats remained close to the shore throughout the entire operation, and were a few yards from the rocks when the shooting began approximately thirty minutes later.

Beaglehole (1974, p.669) states that Cook left the *Resolution* with three boats; his pinnace, the launch and the small cutter. But this contradicts the statements of several of the officers present, including the anonymous writer of the pocket diary (anon., 1779b), and cannot be reconciled with his instructions to Clerke to seal off the bay. To order the placing of boats at the southern end of the bay, and leave the northern end unguarded, would have invited canoes to sail through the gap. Some of the confusion may have been caused by the launch and small cutter leaving the *Resolution* for the north point, and Captain Cook soon after leaving for Kowrowa in the pinnace. Williamson, having placed the small cutter near the rocks, was within shouting distance of Cook in the pinnace as he passed on the way to Kowrowa; the distances between all three boats off the north point would be about a hundred yards. Clerke in his ms. Journal, in reporting his conversation with Lieutenant Gore, says that Gore told him 'that Captain Cook was gone with his Pinnace, Launch and small cutter to a Town situated just within the NW Point'. Beaglehole's misunderstanding of the movements of the boats could have arisen from this.

Meanwhile, Lieutenant King landed at Kakooa at the other end of the bay, and proceeded, according to his official version of the incident, to carry out Captain Cook's last orders to him, which were 'to quiet the minds of the natives, on our side of the bay, by assuring them they shall not be hurt, to keep my people together and to be on my guard'. He goes on: 'My first care, on going ashore, was to give strict orders to the marines to remain within the tent, to load their pieces with ball and not to quit their arms. Afterwards I took a walk to the huts of old Kaoo and the priests, and explained to them, as well as I could, the object of the hostile preparations, which had exceedingly alarmed them. I found, they had already heard of the cutter's being stolen, and I assured them, that though Captain Cook was resolved to recover it, and to punish the authors of the theft, yet that they, and the people of the village on our side, need not be under the smallest apprehension of suffering any evil from us. I desired the priests to explain this to the people, and to tell them not to be alarmed, but to continue peaceable and quiet. Kaoo asked me, with great earnestness, if Terreeoboo was to be hurt? I assured him he was not and both he and the rest of his brethren seemed much satisfied with this assurance' (King, 1784). The image he is creating here is of himself as a pacifier, who by his diplomatic skills achieved what the angry Cook failed to achieve across the bay. In fact for the rest of the morning King presents himself in the published text as the single peace-keeping force in the bay, while everyone else, from Captain Clerke to Master Bligh, was fuelling disaster by ill-considered actions that jeopardised life and ship's property.

But his private Log, written within hours of the tragedy, presents a very different picture. In it he states that after returning to the shore camp he set about making observations with the astronomers: while Captain Cook was ashore King says he was 'in the observatory preparing to take equal altitudes', and it was the gunfire from across the bay that 'so roused & agitated our Spirits, that it was impossible to continue on observing' (King, ms. Log and Proceedings). Measuring altitudes in a detached scientific manner is not consistent with his alleged activities in calming Hawaiians. If, as he emphasises, he knew that Captain Cook had gone ashore to arrest Terreeoboo, then he must have been aware of the dangers involved. Either King was a man of the coolest disposition under stress and excitement, or his published account is inaccurate. As we will see, Lieutenant King under stress was as excitable as anybody else, and therefore his behaviour can be better explained by assuming that he did not know Cook intended to arrest Terreeoboo, but for some reason stated otherwise in his official account.

If King thought Cook had gone ashore merely to bargain with Terreeoboo, then his behaviour as recorded in his private Log makes sense. He was reasonably relaxed because he thought he had no cause to be otherwise. Nobody would attack Cook while he was talking to Terreeoboo, and the small marine party would be enough to deter casual threats to his person. In fact King was not the perceptive commander he made out. He, like everybody else, misread Cook's intentions and the dangers to which he exposed himself. If part of his

1784 version is true, if, that is, the priests and people were alarmed and needed reassurance, then King made a misjudgment. If the gunfire in the bay before Cook went ashore was enough to make the old priests at Kakooa earnestly concerned about Terreeoboo's safety, what would be the reaction of the people of Kowrowa and the large crowds staying there, especially when Lono appeared with armed men in their splendid red uniforms marching through the village? There were serious grounds for alarm at Cook's foray ashore, but King's vigilance was relaxed by Cook's notorious secrecy and failure to think out his action.

If things happened as I have suggested, then Captain Cook was caught in a difficulty of his own making. The seizure of the boats was a hasty and ill-conceived plan which collapsed within minutes as the side-effects of armed blockade became obvious. He failed to inform his officers of his intentions. He did not tell Clerke he was going ashore, because he changed his mind after Clerke had left the ship. He did not tell King that he intended arrest, merely that he was going to visit Terreeoboo and demand the cutter for the canoes. The plan to arrest the King was only half-formed in Cook's mind as he headed for the shore, so he made inadequate preparations for the task he eventually set himself. He went ashore with too weak a force, insufficient reserves, and unbriefed officers in command of the boats. He jumped into something far bigger than he anticipated, and, as we will see, exacerbated his difficulties by unnecessary provocation, secure in the illusion that killing one or two Hawaiians could clear a beach of several thousand hostile men aroused to fever pitch by what they took to be a physical threat to the sacred person of their ruler.

It was impossible for King to make these criticisms of a man rightly renowned in Europe and America for his genius and humanity. And it was a slight to King's own status to admit that Cook did not take him into his confidence about his mission to Kowrowa. I think it most likely that King rewrote his role, and made a retrospective rationalisation of Cook's intentions, running the two plans together to hide the truth. But the failure to face the facts about Captain Cook's deep error of judgment on this occasion meant that the record had to be doctored and scapegoats had to be found.

VI

Cook Thwarted

The timing of events in the next few hours is vague. Each account gives only approximate times, and not all of these can be reconciled. This vagueness is due to the scarcity of pocket watches, and the fact that not much importance was attached at the time to the events leading up to the killings. The most likely time for Cook's landing at Kowrowa is about 7.30 a.m., which best fits the probable times of other events. Cook and Clerke decided on the plan of sealing the bay at about 6.30; it would take time to arrange, as Clerke had to get back to his ship, and the boats had to be manned and positioned. Bligh was sent on his mission at about 7.00, and had completed it before Cook and King left the *Resolution*. Cook was ashore for about thirty minutes before the shooting began, which Clerke times as 8.00 a.m. The action lasted about ten minutes, and by the time the boats returned to the *Resolution* and Lieutenant Williamson reached the *Discovery* it was near 9.00 a.m.

The disposition of his officers and men in the bay when Cook landed is worth noting. With him on shore were Lieutenant Molesworth Phillips and the marine guard. About twenty yards away, the pinnace, under the command of Henry Roberts, was riding at oars. Close to the pinnace was the launch, commanded by Third Lieutenant John Williamson. A short distance from the launch, the *Resolution*'s small cutter, commanded by Lanyon, was patrolling the seaward point with a view to chasing any canoes that put off from the shore. The *Resolution* was about three quarters of a mile from the shore and was commanded by Lieutenant Gore. A few hundred yards to the south of the *Resolution*, the *Discovery* was anchored and under the command of Captain Clerke. The other officer on board was Lieutenant Burney. Burney was in command whenever Clerke left the ship, as he had done twice within the last hour. As we have seen, when Clerke returned from the *Resolution* the second time, he sent his jolly-boat, the last remaining boat on the *Discovery*, to Lieutenant Rickman, who was patrolling the southern point. He does not state whom he sent in command of the jolly-boat. It could have been Burney, but it was more likely to have been one of the Master's Mates or a midshipman; responsibility for what happened later at the southern point was laid at Rickman's door, but it would automatically have been ascribed to Burney, the senior officer, if he had been there.

William Bligh was in charge of the *Resolution*'s large cutter, and we know that he was just off the rocks within the southern point, having finished chasing the canoe, at the moment when Cook left the ship to go ashore. Where was he subsequently? I have dealt on p.43 with Bayly's suggestion that Bligh was with Rickman's blockade party. With the *Discovery*'s three boats between the point and the ship it does not seem likely that Bligh would have remained there after he had completed his task of driving the Hawaiian canoe ashore. He was probably somewhere in the bay between the southern shore-line, where he chased the canoe, and the *Resolution*, during what followed in the next thirty minutes. King says in his ms. Log that 'our boats were scattered about often in chase of Canoes' during this time, and this is probably just what Bligh was doing. It would have been logical for him to take his boat back to the space behind the *Discovery* and the *Resolution*, which was unguarded. This would place him nearer his own ship and the other boats at the north point. We know for certain that he was back on board the *Resolution* when Clerke returned there to take command after Cook's death. Lieutenant King, the astronomers, the carpenters, the sailmakers and six marines (almost certainly including Corporal Ledyard) were at the shore-camp by the morai at Kakooa throughout the entire incident. King had the *Resolution*'s jolly-boat with him and possibly a couple of midshipmen.

Attention has tended to concentrate on what happened to Captain Cook while he was ashore, yet Cook's two plans caused two distinct sets of activities to be under way simultaneously, which were brought together at an important stage in the confrontation between Cook and the Hawaiian chiefs. While Cook was making for the shore, boats from the ships were patrolling the bay watching for escaping canoes. This activity was not stopped after Cook decided on taking the King hostage. As Cook had not told Clerke, or anybody else, of his intentions, there was nobody in a position to recall the boats. Bligh had already completed his chase before Cook left the *Resolution*, and another two canoes were on their way out of the bay at that moment. The ships' big guns had fired at them, according to Lieutenant King, and Lieutenant Rickman and his boats took up positions to give chase at approximately the time when Cook stepped onto the rocks at Kowrowa. The consequences of their chase were to have a bearing on the course of events at Kowrowa, though just how much of a bearing is a matter of controversy.

What happened to Captain Cook at Kowrowa? From the point of view of collecting the evidence this is a difficult question to answer. The *Resolution* was close to the village of Kowrowa but had only one senior officer on board, Lieutenant Gore. All the other officers including the midshipmen were elsewhere in the bay. Gore observed what was happening, presumably by telescope (Gore, ms. Log). On the *Discovery* both Clerke and Burney were observing through their telescopes once the shooting began: Clerke, ms. Journal, 'with my Glass I clearly saw ...'; Burney, ms. Journal, 'with glasses we could see ...'. They were much further away than Gore, though Burney's account suggests that he had a remarkably clear view of the proceedings. He claims to have been able to distinguish Cook from the crowd and also the blow that felled him. Either he had a better quality glass than Clerke – officers supplied their own telescopes and Burney was well off – or he added details on the basis of subsequent information. Lieutenant Rickman was in no position to observe from his position over a mile away (Rickman, ms. Log), and Lieutenant King was also too far away to be able to distinguish what happened (he was not even looking, according to his own Log). Master's Mate Lanyon was about a hundred yards beyond Cook's boat party, and midshipman Trevenen in the boat was unable to see whether Captain Cook was brought off the shore after the shooting began (Lloyd and Anderson, 1959). Henry Roberts wrote an account, but it is surprisingly sparse in detail (Roberts, ms. Log). He was closest to the shore in the pinnace. There is secondary evidence that he doctored his report to remove controversial allegations. Lieutenant Williamson, in the launch, with almost as good a view as Roberts, has not contributed to the historical record, for reasons that will be clearer later. His account was lost, or possibly deliberately destroyed.

The account of what happened in the village, and of subsequent events on the shore, has had to rely mainly on the testimony of only one man, Lieutenant Molesworth Phillips, the marine officer who accompanied Cook ashore. His own written account has been lost. He was interviewed by many officers after the death of Cook, reporting in detail to Captain Clerke and Lieutenant King, who acknowledge his report in their Journals. Other Journals also mention details directly quoted from Phillips (see, for instance, Bligh's account in Gould, 1928b). This has led to some discrepancies in the surviving Journals. Lieutenant King, when he wrote the official version, brought together these accounts and constructed a version consistent with his effort to present Cook's death in a way that did not reflect on his memory (King, 1784); in what follows I have made use of King's version, unscrambling it by reference to the accounts and Journals, particularly Clerke's, which gives a long direct quote from Phillips. All these accounts presumably derive ultimately from Phillips, though Ledyard, being a marine, may have got information from the surviving marines.

According to Phillips, Cook led his party into the village once he had landed on the rocks. The Hawaiians appeared to be as deferential towards Lono as they had always been. Many prostrated themselves and offered gifts to Cook and his men. These gestures were acknowledged by Cook but they did not appear to change his mind about his mission. Ironically they may have reinforced his intentions. That the Hawaiians were behaving with their customary reverence might have indicated to him that his plan to persuade the King to go on board the *Resolution* could be achieved by guile rather than force. If they were trusting to that extent, they might not see any danger to Terreeoboo. But not all the Hawaiians were taken in by Lono's behaviour. This was no ordinary visit. The bay had echoed with the sound of gunfire, and now Lono arrived with red-coated marines, all armed with the strange sticks that the visitors took everywhere with them. Lono generally travelled among the Hawaiians without an escort, while the pinnace waited off shore; the first exception had been the day before, when he took two marines with him to chase the thieves near Kakooa. The bystanders at Kowrowa may not have known what the red-coated men were for, but they associated their parade with trouble. Two boats were riding on oars just off the rocks, and everybody in them had the noisy sticks. Moreover, many of the Hawaiians knew about the stolen boat (King, 1784, noted that the priests at Kakooa knew about it). The arrival in Kowrowa during the night of many people from Kakooa (their absence was noticed by

Lieutenant King) has a sinister aspect to it in retrospect: it is as if they were expecting trouble and wanted to witness the inevitable confrontation. But even if this was not true, it was an error for Cook to believe that he could take Terreeoboo away by guile when he was armed, though not well enough armed to take him by force. Unless Cook adopted his normal reliance on his god-like relationship with the people (which meant in effect coming ashore alone and not with marines) then the mood of the people could only change towards hostility to match the threat to their King, which they would quickly perceive.

Cook asked the villagers he met where King Terreeoboo was. The Hawaiian King did not live in a house that was different from the houses of his subjects; most of the houses looked alike, and could be distinguished mainly by size or age. Cook and his party spent some time marching around the houses looking for the King. Ledyard (1783) writes that Cook 'went by a circuitous march to the house of Teraiobu in order to evade the suspicion of any design. This route led them through a considerable part of the town which discovered every symptom of mischief, though Cook blinded by some fatal cause could not perceive it, or, too self confident would not regard it' (quoted in Munford, 1963a, p.145). The King's sons then appeared, having been brought to Cook by messengers. The questions about Terreeoboo's whereabouts, and the running hither and thither by Hawaiians delighted to oblige Lono, helped raise the level of excitement in the half-awake village. Ledyard further observes (1783, pp. 143-5):

The appearance of our parade both by water and on shore, though conducted with the utmost silence and with as little ostentation as possible, had alarmed the towns on both sides of the bay, but particularly Kiverua, who were in complete order for an onset otherwise it would have been a matter of surprize, that, though Cook did not see 20 men in passing through the town, yet before he had conversed ten minutes with Kireea, he was surrounded by three or four hundred people, and above half of them chiefs.

The walk round the huts may not have helped Cook's patience. He had come ashore for the showdown, and being unable to find the object of his endeavours would have hardened his mood. Another thing told the Hawaiians that something was different that morning; the marines were not stopping off to chatter with them as usual, but were single-minded in their attempts to keep up with Cook and Phillips.

Terreeoboo's sons quickly led Cook to their father's hut. Cook asked the boys to get their father and they went into the hut to tell him that Lono wanted to speak with him. But the King did not immediately appear, so, fearing that he might have escaped into the countryside, Cook sent the Lieutenant into the hut to search it. This in itself was a highly contentious act on Cook's part. Going uninvited into a house belonging to the sovereign of a foreign land was not the most diplomatic way to go about business. It confirms that Cook was in no mood for diplomacy, and also shows him to have been provocative from the beginning. He had stopped the canoes leaving the bay and now he ordered his men to trespass on the King's property. Lieutenant Phillips went into the hut and in one of the rooms found Terreeoboo apparently just awakened from sleep. He asked him to step outside and speak to Captain Cook, which the old King immediately, and allegedly with alacrity, agreed to do.

Clerke's version of Phillips' account of this incident has a different emphasis from some of the others. Clerke writes that Phillips said:

Messengers were immediately dispatch'd and the 2 Boys soon came and conducted us to their Father's house. After waiting some time on the outside Capt Cook doubted the old Gentlemans being there and sent me that I might inform Him. I found our old acquaintance just awoke from Sleep when upon my aquainting him that Capt Cook was at the door, he very readily went with me to Him.

Compare Ledyard's version (Ledyard, 1783):

The Lieutenant went in and found the old man sitting with two or three old women of distinction, and when he gave Kireeaboo to understand that Cook was without and wanted to see him he discovered the greatest marks of uneasiness but arose and accompanied the lieutenant out, holding his hand; when he came before Cook he squatted down upon his hams as a mark of humiliation and Cook took him by the hand from the Lieutenant, and conversed with him.

And Master's Mate Alexander Home says in his ms. Journal:

Captain Cook landed directly and marched through the town, inquiring as he went along for Kuirriaboo, and the people were shy of telling him in what house the king was ... He arrived at last where the King was but he would not come out to him and it was perceived that he had a great number of chiefs about him who were ... restraining him contrary to his inclinations. Upon this Captain Cook ordered Mr Phillips and some of his people to enter the house and persuade him to come out, which they affected but no force was used or any offencive manner.

These accounts are in conflict with that of Clerke and suggest a much more aggressive persuasion of the King to accompany Cook. Sending Phillips (and perhaps some marines) into the hut, taking hold of the King's hand (pulling him along?), and the reported unhappiness of Terreeoboo, if true, would help to explain the rapid rise in tempers on the Hawaiian side. Such behaviour would also be consistent with Cook's mood that morning. Perhaps either Clerke or Phillips glossed over any rough handling to protect Cook's reputation for humanity; though the fact that Terreeoboo appeared compliant until they reached the beach gives them some support.

The King and Cook conversed about the stolen cutter and it was apparent fairly quickly that the theft of the ship's boat was news to Terreeoboo. This must further have confirmed Cook's opinion that the people in this village did not know about the real purpose of his visit. Again he misread the situation. The King was innocent of complicity in the theft of the boat, and could probably have been relied upon to encourage his people to return it, but this was not the same thing as co-operating in using himself as a hostage to force its return. That Terreeoboo had not been wakened by the big guns, or by his people reporting what was going on in the bay, is remarkable, and has never been explained. From the demeanour of Terreeoboo that morning it seems possible that if Cook had thought more clearly from the start, and had not acted so hastily to seal the bay, he might have achieved his goal of using the hostage sanction and got Terreeoboo on board by a normal invitation later in the day. But Cook was acting under the impulse to show the Hawaiians that he was not be be trifled with, and by this he had now placed himself in a difficult situation. He was chatting amicably with Terreeoboo outside the King's house, backed up by a force of armed men, and from this position was attempting to lure the King on board his ship as if they were exchanging gifts on the old friendly basis. Even if the King was too old, or too kind, to read anything sinister into the interview they were having together, several of the chiefs standing around watching were not so sanguine. Other people were arriving all the time, as word spread about Cook's strange behaviour and visit to the King. The anxious thoughts of the old priest at Kakooa, expressed with some agitation to Lieutenant King, were echoed in the minds of the men actually watching the strange performance.

Cook asked Terreeoboo to return with him and board the *Resolution*.

The King agreed without hesitation and his sons were delighted with the chance to go onto the ship. They were frequent visitors on the ships and were trusting regarding Cook's intentions, as was Terreeoboo. He started walking beside Cook, who took his hand and headed for the shore. The King's house was about one hundred yards from the rocky cove where the pinnace was waiting. The King's sons, unsuspecting, raced on ahead of the procession and swam out to the pinnace. They sat for some minutes in the boat with Roberts waiting for their father and Lono. Cook and Terreeoboo appeared in the midst of a large crowd of Hawaiians, now several thousand in number, a few yards from the rocks. That the King and his sons felt they had nothing at all to fear from Cook is shown by their co-operation up to this point in the proceedings.

From Cook's point of view everything was going well. Lieutenant King wrote (1784):

Things were in this prosperous train, the two boys being already in the pinnace, and the rest of the party being advanced near the water side, when an elderly woman called *Kanee-kabareea*, the mother of the boys, and one of the King's favourite wives, came after him, and with many tears, and entreaties, besought him not to go on board. At the same time, two chiefs, who came along with her, laid hold of him, and insisting, that he should go no farther, forced him to sit down. The natives, who were collecting in prodigious numbers, along the shore, and had probably been alarmed by the firing of the great guns, and the appearances of hostility in the bay, began to throng around Captain Cook and their King.

The Hawaiians were not unanimous in their opinions about Captain Cook's intentions towards their King. The hostility that developed against him in the next minutes started with a small group of Hawaiians led by some of Terreeoboo's immediate entourage. Whether the two chiefs mentioned by Lieutenant King deliberately provoked Terreeoboo's wife to act the way she did, we cannot say. The incidents of the previous day between Hawaiians and the seamen indicate hostility towards the visitors among some of the Hawaiians, but this was not enough to explain the emotional atmosphere that quickly developed at Kowrowa. However, the conditions for emotional misunderstanding were present at this moment, and it must be said that Captain Cook's behaviour had contributed to them in no small measure.

The intervention of Kanee-Kabareea and the physical restraint of

Tereeoboo by the two chiefs altered the situation immediately. The Hawaiian King was now sitting down and all the other participants were standing up, volubly arguing and gesticulating. The peaceful option was cancelled. Captain Cook, bending down, spent some time urging Terreeoboo to come with him, while the chiefs, in a similar posture, pressed the opposite point of view. The crowd was growing more excited as the row went on between Lono and their chiefs, and the marines were standing helplessly while the crowd pressed round them to get a better view of what was going on.

Should Cook have abandoned his mission at this point? Discretion might have suggested that he should, since there was now no chance of getting Terreeoboo aboard by guile. Cook did not appear to accept this argument. He continued with his appeals to Terreeoboo. But in doing so, he proved the case of the chiefs who were telling the King that Cook meant to harm him. As long as no visible force was threatened, and it seemed possible to decline, there could be some pretence that the invitation to go on board the ship was a friendly gesture; but the pretence had to be dropped as soon as it was obvious that Cook was insisting excitedly on the King's acceptance of the invitation.

That Captain Cook's temper was rising we know from Phillips' report. Phillips was growing apprehensive. He and his marines were surrounded by jostling Hawaiians, and had no room to present their arms if the need arose. Captain Cook was several paces in front of the nearest marines, almost alone with the King and the principal parties to the argument. Phillips advised Captain Cook to leave the King and embark on the boats. He was unable to persuade Cook to accept this advice. Cook seemed determined to force the issue. He was not going to be thwarted easily, and may have been so absorbed in trying to persuade Terreeoboo to acknowledge his entreaties that he was oblivious to the size and the mood of the crowd about him. For his part, Terreeoboo 'seemed entirely resigned to the will of others', sat with his head down on his chest and 'appeared much distressed' (Samwell, 1786; Kippis, 1842, p.374). Burney, in his ms. Journal, says that he 'seemed irresolute and frighten'd', Clerke (quoting Phillips) that 'the old man now appear'd dejected and frighten'd'.

Since he was unable to persuade Cook to desist, Phillips spoke to Cook: 'Well Sir says he Shall I draw up the Marines close to the Waters' edge in order to secure a retreat for I see plainly by the

Indians actions it will become necessary, the Captn reply'd that there was no occasion, but that he might if he wou'd, and seem'd to grant it because the other had ask'd it' (from Harvey's ms. Log). Phillips had less faith in Captain Cook's ability to handle the situation than Cook had, and he was more realistic about the dangers now present. The crowd were visibly hostile and some of them were appearing with spears and wooden knives. According to Samwell (1786) 'Indians' had been seen arming themselves and putting on their war-mats even before Terreeoboo left the village. The isolated abuse was now rising to a general shout. Phillips took his Captain's reply to be an order to re-form his marines, and accordingly gave the orders to Sergeant Gibson. The crowd around the marines gave without resistance, and allowed the marines pass between them and assemble in a line along the rocks by the water's edge (Clerk, ms. Journal). This left Captain Cook, Lieutenant Phillips and Sergeant Gibson several paces into the crowd and separated from the line of marines. These three stood in a line with Cook at one end.

By now even Captain Cook could see that his attempt to get Terreeoboo on board the *Resolution* was a total failure. He could not persuade the King to accompany him as long as the chiefs argued the opposite point of view. They were telling the King that he would be killed if he went with Cook. This probably made Cook even angrier: he had no intention of killing Terreeoboo, and probably took such suggestions as a personal insult. As the arguments went back and forward with no movement in either side's intentions, so tempers were fuelled. Cook was furious at his failure and barely controlled himself. He turned to Phillips and, according to Clerke, said: 'We can never think of compelling him to go onboard without killing a number of these People.' This statement can be taken in two ways, to imply either that he was prepared to kill and thought that this was now the only way to succeed, or that he baulked at killing and was acknowledging the failure of his mission and attempting to rationalise the decision to retreat. Either way, what made him think killing anybody at this stage would get Terreeoboo on board is difficult to imagine. As the source of the Hawaiian anger was a belief that Cook was going to kill their King, it would not help his case to confirm them in that opinion by killing somebody else. At the base of his statement was his persistent belief that one shot would clear the beach, or at least that killing one or two Hawaiians would enable him to do what he wanted. Another possibility is that Phillips attributed these words to Cook in a misguided attempt to make his Commander's behaviour appear in a better light.

Faced with the realisation that his mission was a failure, there was only one thing Cook could do, and that was to embark and leave the shore. His second plan had been no more successful than the first. The stolen boat was still missing and he had got no further towards recovering it. He would have to return to the *Resolution* empty-handed and without tangible means of recovering the boat. The Hawaiians had got the upper hand once again.

VII

The Death of Captain Cook

For a few minutes after it became clear to him that Terreeoboo was not going to leave Kowrowa voluntarily, it was probably still possible for Cook to have retreated safely. A number of factors conspired to prevent this relatively happy ending to the confrontation. Decisive action on Cook's part would have settled the matter, but he hesitated. He was not used to being thwarted, either by his own men or by Polynesians. To leave Kowrowa without Terreeoboo was unpalatable enough, but to leave without some semblance of dignity was unthinkable. He had come ashore for a showdown, and was now facing defeat without having impressed the Hawaiians with his superior technology. So he delayed a few fatal minutes while searching for some way of saving his face. As Harvey says (ms. Log): 'The Captn instead of repairing to the Boats as he was urg'd to do, but permitted the greatest insults from them ... by an infatuation that is altogether unaccountable continued to trifle away his time on shore.'

While his words to Phillips may indicate acknowledgment of failure and the decision to retreat, this retreat was not understood by the Hawaiians. Cook wanted to leave with dignity, but those Hawaiians who were most opposed to his presence on the island, and who saw his behaviour as threatening their King, had no intention of letting him leave without a public exhibition of their hostility. His retreat was taken as a proof of his weakness, and weakness in a chief was for the Hawaiians contemptible. Though Cook could still have got off the shore without physical harm, he had no chance of leaving without suffering visible signs of Hawaiian contempt. This conspired with Cook's famous personal failing, namely his savage temper, to prevent him ever leaving the shore.

The sequence of events in the next few minutes was described by Lieutenant King in the official version in a way that serves to gloss over the interchange between Captain Cook and the Hawaiians nearest to him. This is in keeping with King's intention of absolving Cook from much of the responsibility for his own death. King wrote (1784):

Though the enterprise, which had carried Captain Cook on shore had now failed, and was abandoned, yet his person did not appear to have been in the least danger, till an accident happened, which gave a fatal turn to the affair. The boats, which had been stationed across the bay, having fired at some canoes, that were attempting to get out, unfortunately had killed a Chief of the first rank. The news of his death arrived at the village where Captain Cook was, just as he had left the King, and was walking slowly towards the shore. The ferment it occasioned was very conspicuous; the women and children were immediately sent off; and the men put on their war-mats, and armed themselves with spears and stones.

It is this passage which inspired Hough (1972) to erect his shaky argument that the young Bligh indirectly caused Cook's death.

In fact it was Lieutenant Rickman's boat party at the southern point which had fired on the canoes and killed a chief. This was the chase which had begun just as Cook left the *Resolution* for the shore. In his Log King says that Cook spoke to Phillips about the gunfire which killed the chief immediately before the mass attack on him: '[Cook] express'd his apprehensions of our situation at the Observatorys; observing to him, that I was very weak in force, & he thought that he heard some Muskets from our quarter & that we were attack'd. These Muskets were fir'd by Mr Rickmans party, who were in boats at the Soermost part of the bay, keeping in the Canoes, in doing so they killd a Very principal Chief.' It is not clear when Cook heard the gunfire. Most of the evidence suggests that the chief was killed some time before the firing began on shore and Cook was attacked. This makes it less likely that the news was the decisive factor. Burney (ms. Journal) writes:

Captain Cook had scarcely got on shore, when the boats near the south part of the harbour fired several muskets at some large canoes that were trying to. get out, by which an Indian chief, named Kareemoo, was killed. The first notice we had of this was from two Indians who came off to the two ships in a small canoe to complain of it, but finding they were not attended to, they enquired for Captain Cook; being told he was at the town of Kowrowa, they went thither. About 1/2 an hour after this we heard the firing of muskets on shore, which was followed by the *Resolution*'s pinnace and launch firing.

Edgar's account is similar: while Cook was ashore in the village, a small canoe with two Hawaiians in it drew abreast of the *Discovery* to tell them that a chief had been killed. The people on the *Discovery* 'took no notice of what they said but laughed at them'. The Hawaiians then went across to the *Resolution* to ask for Cook, but 'finding with much the same satisfaction they got from us, they went ashore to the town of Kowrowa where Captain Cook was' (Edgar, ms. Log). Captain Clerke's account specifically denies that the news of the death was what caused the attack on Cook: 'Sometime before the attack was made, intelligence was brought from the other side of the bay, that the Boats there under the command of Lt Rickman had killed a man who was somewhat of an Aree, which our People observed seemed in some degree to disconcert them, but this was some time before they proceeded to violent measures.'

According to Samwell (quoted in Kippis, 1842, pp. 373-4) the news of the chief's death arrived while Terreeoboo was still outside his house conversing with Captain Cook, before he was stopped by his wife and before the altercation developed, and was not therefore the immediate trigger for the violent assault, though it increased the apprehension of the Hawaiians.

In a little time, however, the Indians were observed arming themselves with long spears, clubs and daggers, and putting on thick mats, which they use as armour. This hostile appearance increased, and became more alarming, on the arrival of two men in a canoe from the opposite side of the bay, with the news of a chief, called Kareemoo, having been killed by one of the *Discovery*'s boats. In their passage across, they had also delivered this account to each of the Ships. Upon that information, the women who were sitting upon the beach at their breakfasts, and conversing familiarly with our people in the boats, retired, and a confused murmour spread through the crowd.

Against this, and coinciding with King, we have the anonymous officer on the *Resolution*, and the accounts of the Rev. William Ellis and of Ledyard, who make the incident the dramatic turning-point. The officer (anon., 1779b) writes:

About this time a Canoe from the opposite shore came alongside both ships and informed us that an Aree from Noo-Numa was killed by a musket from one of the *Discovery*'s boats; from the ships he went ashore where the Capt. then was and there repeated the same; this I am told determined what before they seemed rather wavering about and the women and children began to march up the hills; this we could see from the ships, their situation on shore then became alarming and hostility appeared not far off, the Capt. expressed much concern for the party on shore with the observatory fore mast, fearing they were too weak. The Capt.s party was then totally surrounded by the natives.

In contrast to this cautious account (the officer says he 'was told' that the news was decisive), Ledyard links the death of the chief directly with Cook's firing at a Hawaiian (Ledyard, 1783, p.145):

Some of the crowd now cried out that Cook was trying to take their king from them and kill him, and there was one in particular that advanced towards Cook in an attitude that alarmed one of the guard, who presented his bayonet and opposed him, Acquainting Cook in the meantime of the danger of his situation, and that the Indian in a few minutes would attack him, that he had overheard the man whom he had just stopped from rushing in upon him say that our boats which were out in the harbour had just killed his brother, and he would be revenged. Cook attended to what the man said, and desired him to shew him the Indian that had dared to attempt a combat with him, and as soon as he was pointed out Cook fired at him with a blank. The Indian perceiving he received no damage from the fire rushed from without the crowd a second time, and threatened any one that should appose him. Cook perceiving this fired a ball, which entering the Indian's groin he fell and was drawn off by the rest.

The Rev. William Ellis gives an even more dramatic account (1974, pp. 131-2), supposedly told to him by Hawaiians.

While [Terreeoboo] was hesitating, a man came running from the other side of the bay, entered the crowd almost breathless, and exclaimed, '*It is war!* – the foreigners have commenced hostilities, have fired on a canoe from one of their boats, and killed a chief'. This enraged some of our people, and alarmed the chiefs, as they feared Captain Cook would kill the king. The people armed themselves with stones, clubs and spears. All the chiefs did the same. The king sat down.

He says that his account agreed in the 'main facts with the account published by Captain King', and he was probably influenced to some extent by King's account when he interpreted what the Hawaiians had told him.

Even if members of Kareemoo's family were present among the crowd, it is doubtful whether this was sufficient to cause the attack on Cook. The two Hawaiians were seeking out Cook to lay their complaint before him. They did not intend to punish him themselves, but to ask him to punish Rickman (hence their visits to the ships). Cook as Lono was a god, and a front-rank chief; the prerogative of killing was firmly believed by Hawaiians to belong to chiefs. On countless occasions before, Polynesians had indicated that capital punishment was perfectly understandable to them. They did not like deliberate cruelty, such as flogging; for them punishment was a speedy action – a strong blow on the skull with a heavy club. They understood that a man should be punished for offending a chief, and by punishment they meant the death penalty. For instance Parea the previous evening had asked Edgar if Cook would kill him for what happened during their altercation. This makes it less likely that the attack on Cook was motivated by desire for revenge for the death of Kareemoo. The two Hawaiians who brought the news did not find Cook, but the news soon passed through the crowd and would have served to excite the Hawaiians still more, and to confirm the accusations of the agitators among them about Cook's intentions, while a further incident was needed to spark off the attack.

Lono's actions were intelligible to the Hawaiians only within the context of their culture. They had no conception of the importance to Lono of the loss of a boat, or of the bluff he intended in taking Terreeoboo hostage. The arguments between Cook and the chiefs about Terreeoboo's visit to the *Resolution* were reported by those nearest the front of the crowd to those behind who could not see what was going on. It was seldom that one chief killed another chief without a war, and for Lono to think of harming Terreeoboo outside war was incomprehensible to them. If Lono was at war with them, they had to get ready for battle. But Lono as a god could make new rules; gods when angry made human sacrifices, killed people and stripped their bones of flesh. Some men were shouting, others were arming and others did not know what to do. It was sufficiently frightening for the women and children to melt away. Cook as Lono was the key to the Hawaiian understanding of what was going on, and he had to make the first move. He obliged them in the most dramatic of ways: he killed a man before their eyes.

The official version of what happened at this point is unsatisfactory. Lieutenant King has left something out. Even if King's statement is taken at face value, then Captain Cook is far from exculpated from blame for what followed. King wrote (1784):

One of the natives having in his hands a stone, and a long iron spike (which they called a *Pahooa*) came up to the Captain, flourishing his weapons, by way of defiance, and threatening to throw a stone. The Captain desired him to desist; but the man persisting in his insolence, he was at length provoked to fire a load of small-shot. The man having his mat on, which the shot was not able to penetrate, this had no other effect than to irritate and encourage them. Several stones were thrown at the marines; and one of the Erees attempted to stab Mr Phillips with his *pahooa*; but failed in the attempt, and received from him a blow with the but end of his musket. Captain Cook now fired his second barrel, loaded with ball, and killed one of the foremost natives. A general attack with stones immediately followed, which was answered by a discharge of musketry from the marines, and the people in the boats. The islanders, contrary to the expectations of every one, stood the fire with great firmness; and before the marines had time to reload, they broke in upon them with dreadful shouts and yells. What followed was a scene of the utmost horror and confusion.

The picture created here is one in which the normally humane Captain Cook is provoked by an excited Hawaiian into firing a warning shot. The fact that Cook fired his barrel of small shot, it is implied, shows that he did not at first intend to kill the man. But as the small shot failed to penetrate at all, instead of stopping his insolence, it led to a general assault on the marines by the crowd with stones. This then provoked the marines and Captain Cook to use ball shot which killed. King goes on to show how, in his view, Captain Cook's humanity was the final cause of his death: when the marines and the boats opened fire, apparently without orders, Cook called to them to cease firing and was stabbed and clubbed while his back was turned. King writes (1784):

Our unfortunate commander, the last time he was seen distinctly, was standing at the water's edge, and calling out to the boats to cease firing, and to pull in. If it be true, as some of those who were present have imagined, that the marines and the boat-men fired without his orders, and that he was desirous of preventing any further bloodshed, it is not improbable, that his humanity, on this occasion, proved fatal to him. For it was remarked, that whilst he faced the natives, none of them had offered him any violence, but that having turned about, to give his orders to the boats, he was stabbed in the back, and fell with his face into the water.

If we examine in detail the various accounts of what happened, including what Phillips told Captain Clerke and others, another more plausible sequence of events emerges: Cook was threatened and insulted, shot a man dead with the intention of inhibiting the

Hawaiians and revenging himself for the insolence, and this provoked the assault – making King's insistence on Cook's 'humanity' sound rather hollow.

Something happened before Cook fired which King has left out of the official account: a Hawaiian threw something at Captain Cook which struck him on the face. Some versions say it was a stone; Bayly says it was breadfruit (ms. Log and Journal): 'They begun to be very insolent & one of them threw some Bread fruit against Capt Cook's face for which the Capt gave him a punch on the Breast with the butt of his double barrel'd gun.' The accounts of the killing of the Hawaiian differ, and in particular it is not clear just which Hawaiian Cook shot dead. Some have him firing at the man who threw something at him instead of merely repelling him with his butt-end; some have him actually killing him, Ledyard for instance: 'Cook was hit with a stone, and perceiving the man who hove, shot him dead' (Ledyard, 1783, p.146). Some have assumed that the man who received the small shot on his war mat was the one shot dead with the second barrel; but Phillips, according to Clerke, separates the two. Captain Cook, he says, 'I believe was just going to give the orders to embark, when he was interrupted by a fellow arm'd with a long Iron spike (which they call a Pah'hoo'ah) and a Stone; this Man made a flourish with his Pah'hoo'ah, and threatened to throw his stone upon which Capt Cook discharg'd a load of small shot at him but having his Mat on the small shot did not penetrate it, and had no other effect than further to provoke and encourage them.' Phillips' attention at this moment was diverted by another Hawaiian trying to stab him and he says some stones were being thrown, one of which knocked down a marine. He says that 'The Capt then fir'd a ball and kill'd a Man' but does not give details.

King followed Clerke's account closely in his official version, quoted above; again the firing of the barrel of small shot at the man with the spear and the stone is separated from the firing of the barrel of ball, and it is not specified whether the target on each occasion was the same man. Samwell's account, the most detailed, gives more or less the same story, with a motive for shooting the second man dead; in his version two Hawaiians are killed, and he includes an attack by a chief which shows Cook trying to avoid killing. He also gives Cook's remark, reported by Phillips, that he could not take Terreeoboo without loss of life:

A Chief, well known to us, of the name of Coho, was observed lurking near, with an iron dagger, partly concealed under his cloak, seemingly with the intention of stabbing Captain Cook, or the lieutenant of marines. The latter proposed to fire at him but Captain Cook would not permit it. Coho, closing upon them, obliged the officer to strike at him with his piece, which made him retire ... Captain Cook seeing the tumult increase, and the Indians growing more daring and resolute, observed, that if he were to take the king by force, he could not do it without sacrificing the lives of many of his people. He then paused a little, and was on the point of giving orders to re-embark, when a man threw a stone at him, which he returned with a discharge of small shot (with which one barrel of his double piece was loaded). The man, having a thick mat before him, received little or no hurt, he brandished his spear, and threatened to dart it at Captain Cook, who being still unwilling to take away his life, instead of firing with ball, knocked him down with his musket. He expostulated strongly with the most forward of the crowd, upon their turbulent behaviour ... One man was observed behind a double canoe, in the action of darting his spear at Captain Cook, who was forced to fire at him in his own defence, but happened to kill another close to him equally forward in the tumult, the sergeant observing that he had missed the man aimed at, received orders to fire at him, which he did and killed him. (Samwell, quoted in Kippis, 1842, pp. 375-6).

The sequence of events is corroborated by others (Law, Edgar and Harvey for example), though different details are given. Edgar links the shooting directly with the stone-throwing and Cook's rage at the Hawaiians' insolent behaviour (ms. Log):

A man more officious than the rest in getting him [Terreeoboo] back to his house was exceedingly saucy and behaved in a very insolent manner to Captain Cook who gave him a load of small shot. At this the natives took no notice, but laughed and threw stones, which so enraged the Capt that he shot a man dead with ball, having a double barrelled gun, he being told by the Searg he had shot the wrong man, he then told him to shoot the right, this accident happened, made the natives prepare with their daggers and spears to revenge the death of the men, one of them I believe was an Aree.

While we cannot be sure exactly why Cook shot a Hawaiian dead, these accounts make it almost certain that his act preceeded the general onrush of the crowd. Clerke makes the sensible comment; 'Upon the whole I firmly believe matters would not have been carried to the extremities they were had not Capt Cook attempted to chastize a man in the midst of this multitude, firmly believing as his last resource, in case of necessity that the fire of his Marines would undoubtedly disperse them.' Though the suggestion that he fired in self-defence cannot be ruled out, it is likely from what we know of Cook's character, and from the evidence, that he fired with the deliberate intention of making an example of the latest Hawaiian to trespass on his famous short temper.[1]

When Captain Cook shot the Hawaiian dead, the crowd responded almost immediately. Terreeoboo's two young sons, sitting in the pinnace with Roberts, became frightened and asked to be put ashore. Sergeant Gibson was told to fire at a Hawaiian who was judged to be causing trouble, and Phillips was attacked by a chief who tried to stab him with a pahooa. Phillips hit his arm aside and, reversing his musket, butt-ended him. Hawaiians within the crowd hurled stones over the heads of their countrymen into the small space where Captain Cook and his men were pressed. At least one struck a target; a marine fell after being hit by a heavy stone.

It is not clear if the marines received orders to fire (Phillips, unlike King in his Log and Proceedings, says that Captain Cook ordered this personally) but that a smart fire was necessary·at this moment is incontestable. The marines opened fire with a single volley into the crowd, killing some Hawaiians, but this did not halt the rush; those at the front were impelled by those behind, and the dead and dying were trampled on. The marine guard showed their lack of discipline at this crucial moment. No sooner had they emptied their muskets than they dropped them and splashed into the water. Those that could not swim tried; those that could made for the pinnace. They left behind their weapons, which were all captured by the Hawaiians. They also left behind Captain Cook, Lieutenant Phillips, Sergeant Gibson and those marines who could not swim.

The general volley brought Roberts and his crew into the picture (Roberts, ms. Log). They had been resting on their oars waiting for orders a few yards from the shore during the entire time that Cook was ashore. They had apparently not been alarmed at what was happening up to the moment when Cook and the marines fired. After

---

[1] In support of this we have evidence from an interesting letter (Christopher Keest to J.E. Taylor, 4 April 1849, Dixson Library Ms, Sydney) regarding Phillips' missing ms. Keest loaned the ms. to Taylor and wrote: 'I sent you last night by our James Lt.Col. Molesworth Phillips MS of Capt. Cooke's last Voyage … Pray, take care of the Book, You will find Phillips' account of the death of Capt Cooke interesting I think, p.88, seq. as it shows that *he* (not the islanders) was the assailant.' (Quoted in Beaglehole, 1955-69, p. clxxvi).

the firing ('which was seconded by the boats' – Roberts, ms. Log) and the immediate about-turn of most of the marines into the water, Roberts moved the pinnace closer to where Cook was. But a handful of men firing in the general direction of the crowd was not sufficient to stop the onslaught. Reloading a musket in a moving boat is not the easiest of tasks even for trained men. It was made even harder by the arrival of the survivors among the marines. In getting into the boat they rocked it even more. Trying to keep the boat off the rocks and stop it from capsizing, while making room for the marines, made systematic firing of muskets impossible. They were also hampered by the flying stones; and there was a danger that if they got too close in, 'Indians' would swim out and capsize the boats. Harvey (quoted in Beaglehole, 1955-69, vol. 3, p.536) says 'no sooner were the Marines pieces discharg'd when the Boats began and did great execution', but this can only have been with the first volley. For much of the next deadly few minutes they were ineffective.

The volley did not, however, bring Lieutenant Williamson into the fray. Astonishingly, his boat kept to its station more distant from the shoreline, and did not make any attempt to pick up marines from the water. Instead it moved away out of range of the stones. Most accounts – as for example Harvey and Roberts above – refer to fire from the 'boats', but Williamson's conduct during this exchange was not, as we shall see, consistent with his men firing at the shore. Lanyon's boat with the midshipmen in it did engage in the latter part of the action and fired muskets, and the references to 'boats' could indicate Roberts and Lanyon in the pinnace and small cutter. The question of Williamson's failure to take action, and the violent recriminations that followed in the aftermath to Cook's death, is discussed in the next chapter.

On shore the position was hopeless. Cook had no weapon; his double-barrelled gun was empty. Phillips reported (Clerke, ms. Journal) that he had fired 'just after the Capt and loaded again whilst the Marines fir'd'. It took a good soldier a few seconds to load and fire: they could get about two shots a minute from their muskets. The fact that the marines did not reload suggests that the Hawaiians were upon them the second their muskets were fired. When they fled into the sea they left Cook undefended against the attacking crowd. He could not swim, and could not get into the pinnace unless it came right up to the rocks.

The accounts of Cook's last orders and the last few moments of his life are confused. According to Phillips, as reported by Clerke, Cook was almost in the water and shouted 'Take to the Boats'. This seems rather a pointless order, as most of the marines were already in the water. It is unlikely, also, that he would have ordered the men to the boats and thus left himself undefended. Phillips may have invented this order to justify his men's desertion after firing their muskets; it also justifies his following them into the water. 'Almost instantaneously' Phillips continues 'upon my repeating the Orders to take to the Boats I was knock'd down by a stone and in rising receiv'd a Stab with a Pah'hoo'ah in the shoulder; my Antagonist was just on the point of seconding his blow when I shot him dead.' Phillips now had an empty weapon, though he still had his officer's sword. However, he continues his report to Clerke (adopted by Lieutenant King in his 1784 account):

The business was now a most miserable scene of confusion – the Shouts and Yells of the Indians far exceeded all the noise I ever came in the way of these fellows instead of retiring upon being fir'd at, as Capt Cook and I believe, most People concluded they would, acted so very contrary a part, that they never gave the Soldiers time to reload their Pieces, but immediately broke in upon and would have kill'd every man of them had not the Boats by a smart fire kept them a little off and pick'd up those who were not too much wounded to reach them. After being knock'd down I saw no more of Capt Cook, all my People I observed were totally vanquish'd and endeavouring to save their lives by getting to the Boats – I therefore scrambled as well as I could into the Water and made for the Pinnace which I fortunately got hold of, but not before I receiv'd another blow from a stone just above the Temple which, had not the Pinnace been very near would have sent me to the Bottom.

Phillips makes no mention of using his sword, although Hough (1972) has him gallantly defending himself sword in hand.

Phillips did not see Cook again after he was knocked down, though up to this point they were only a few paces from each other, near enough, supposedly, for Cook to give him the order to take to the boats. Cook was close to the water's edge and presumably tried to get closer to it with the intention of getting into the pinnace. If the Hawaiians were attacking the marines, they must have been all round Cook, because the marines had been nearer the water than he had a few moments earlier. Thus, in these crucial seconds between the firing by the marines and their getting into the pinnace, Captain Cook was alone, and armed only with his empty piece which he could swing at his attackers. Yet some accounts have it that in this situation Captain Cook, with the utmost disregard for his personal safety, waved to the boats an order to cease firing.

That Cook turned towards the boats and waved his arm or hat at them is believable, but I think the only credible interpretation of his signal is that he was calling the boats further in so that he and the remaining men could be taken off. That it was an order to cease firing (Roberts, Samwell, Watts, King) is unbelievable. Williamson even argued that he thought Captain Cook was signalling to him to move his boat further out; he does not explain why Cook wanted this, but uses the supposed order to justify his actions in doing precisely that – he moved his boat further off the shore (Kippis, 1842, p.376). I think it likely that both Roberts and Williamson misunderstood the order in such a way as to justify their own conduct. Williamson decided Captain Cook meant. him to pull out because this is what he in fact did, and Roberts took his signal as an order to cease firing because this is what in fact happened in his boat. Roberts says 'The Captain immediately gave orders to cease firing and come in with the boats', suggesting that he understood the real meaning of the signal. King says in his Log: 'It is said by some that he now ordered the Marines to fire & which was followed by the boats, others that the boats fir'd first, & the reason why they did so, was that some of the Indians were observed coming behind the Marines & going to strike them with their Iron daggers, upon which some of the men in the boats fyrd without orders. Be that as it may, the Captn called on them to cease fyring.' Harvey's version is as follows: '... when being waved to come in to take them off, those in the Boats thought it was to desist from firing which they did as they were rowing towards the shore, which the Indians immediately perceived, and before the boats cou'd take them off they rush'd in upon them knock'd down the Captn, the Corporal and four private Marines.'[2]

---

[2] Lanyon (ms. Log) states that the boats fired while Cook was leaving the King and walking to the water's edge: 'He immediately in a great passion call'd to them to disist & come in, intending to enbark as fast as possible. His humanity at this time cost him his life.' King appears to have lifted the last sentence (King, 1784). Roberts' and Williamson's boats were between Lanyon and the shore and he himself says that he could not see whether Cook was taken off. It is unlikely that he was able to see what happened before the boats fired. See also Martin, ms. Journal. Martin was in the launch with Williamson.

According to. most accounts Cook was left standing on the rocks waving to the boats to come in and pick him up. His back was, of course, towards the Hawaiians and one of them struck him high in the back with a heavy club. This knocked him to his knees and another Hawaiian stabbed him in the neck with his pahooa. He fell face forward into the water. The excited crowd surged over the rocks and dagger blows landed all over Captain Cook's prostrate body. He was held under water by some of his attackers while others stabbed him repeatedly. The irregular firing from the pinnace was now not sufficient to deter his attackers, and the men in the boat, while only a few yards from their captain, had to watch helpless as the Hawaiians dragged his lifeless body out of the water and on to the rocks. With him were four of the marines who had been unable to get away. They too were clubbed and stabbed to death.

Edgar and Law, neither of whom was present (both were on the *Discovery*), have a different account of Cook's last moments, in which after being knocked down from behind with a club to his knees, Cook 'immediately got up and rashly went alone into the middle of the crowd following the man, who he beat with the butt end of his piece' (Edgar, ms. Log). Phillips does not report this incident, but he lost sight of Cook when he was knocked down. Cook may have tried to defend himself with his piece, but it is more likely that Edgar and Law are confusing Cook's final struggle with the earlier incident when a man threw breadfruit and Cook responded, according to King's Log, 'with the butt end of his piece', and followed his assailant into the crowd.

Samwell, who was not an eyewitness at Kowrowa, wrote the most detailed account of Cook's dying moments, and it is worth quoting here for its dramatic effectiveness (Samwell, 1786). As Phillips claims he was separated from Cook at the moment of his death, Samwell's account must have been based on information from Roberts or Williamson, but it probably contains a fair dose of imaginative reconstruction:

Captain Cook was then the only one remaining on the rock: he was observed making for the pinnace, holding his left hand against the back of his head, to guard it from the stones, and carrying his musket under the other arm. An Indian was seen following him, but with caution and timidity; for he stopped once or twice, as if undetermined to proceed. At last he advanced upon him unawares, and with a large club, or common stake, gave him a blow on the back of the head, and then precipitately retreated. The stroke seemed to have stunned Captain Cook: he staggered a few paces then fell on his hand and one knee, and dropped his musket. As he was rising, and before he could recover his feet, another Indian stabbed him in the back of the neck with an iron dagger. He then fell into a bit of water about knee deep, where others crowded upon him, and endeavoured to keep him under: but struggling very strongly with them, he got his head up, and casting his look towards the pinnace, seemed to solicit assistance. Though the boat was not above five or six yards distant from him, yet from the crowded and confused state of the crew, it seems, it was not in their power to save him. The Indians got him under again, but in deeper water; he was, however, able to get his head up once more, and being almost spent in the struggle, he naturally turned to the rock, and was endeavouring to support himself by it, when a savage gave him a blow with a club and he was seen alive no more. They hauled him lifeless on the rocks, where they seemed to take a savage pleasure in using every barbarity to his dead body, snatching daggers out of each others hand, to have the horrid satisfaction of piercing the fallen victim of their barbarous rage.

VIII

The Aftermath

'The whole affair from [the O]pening to the End did [not] last 10 Minutes, or [was] their a spark of cour[age] or Conduct shown in [the] whole busyness' (quoted in Gould, 1928b). This was William Bligh's summing up of the conduct of Captain Cook's marine guard and boat crews. Even allowing for Bligh's acid contempt for Lieutenants Williamson and Phillips there is more than a grain of truth in his conclusion. The facts are hardly in dispute. The marines did desert their captain, and the so-called 'smart fire' (King, 1784) from the boats was intermittent at its most intense. What happened in those ten minutes caught many people by surprise. It took some time for the tragedy to sink in, and very soon afterwards recriminations began to flow.

Captain Clerke's Journal tells us the approximate time that Cook died. He wrote: 'It was now just 8 O'clock when we were alarm'd by the discharge of a Volley of small Arms from Capt Cook's People and a violent Shout of the Indians; with my Glass I clearly saw that our People were drove off to their Boats but I could not distinguish Persons in the confused Crowd; the Pinnace and Launch however continued the fire and the *Resolution* who was near enough to throw her shot onshore fir'd her Cannon among them.' His First Lieutenant, James Burney, standing with him on the *Discovery*, must have had a better telescope: 'With Glasses we could see Captn Cook receive a Blow from a Club and fall off a Rock into the Water. The ships then fired, but at too great a distance to make sure of any particular mark.' Burney was mistaken in saying that both ships fired their great guns at Kowrowa. Only the *Resolution* was near enough; the *Discovery* later fired at the Kakooa shore camp.

Several accounts, King's particularly, single out Lieutenant Phillips of the marines for special praise and credit him with the status of the hero of the moment. King wrote (1784):

The rest, with Mr. Phillips, their Lieutenant, threw themselves into the water, and escaped, under cover of a smart fire from the boats. On this occasion, a remarkable instance of gallant behaviour, and of affection for his men was shown by the officer. For he had scarcely got into the boat, when seeing one of the marines, who was a bad swimmer, struggling in the water, and in danger of being taken by the enemy, he immediately jumped into the sea to his assistance, though much wounded himself; and after receiving a blow on the head from a stone, which had nearly sent him to the bottom, he caught the man by the hair and brought him safe off.

The marines, instead of being heavily censured for their disorderly retreat, are relieved of all criticism, and what little glory is available for distribution is concentrated upon Phillips, their officer. Bligh was furious at this development, and contemptuously described Phillips' story about how he killed his assailant as 'a most infamous li[e]'. He also contradicts King on the gallant rescue of the marine by Phillips, stating that 'the Man was close to the Boat & swam nearly as well as the Lieut.' (Gould, 1928b). Bligh had no doubts about who was to blame for Cook's death. 'The Marines fire[d] & ran,' he wrote on a copy of King (1784), 'which occasioned al[l] that followed for had the[y] fixed their bayonets & not have run, so frighte[ned] as the[y] were, they might have drove all before t[hem].' He was the only observer to place the blame squarely on the marines.

If Phillips' role is at least in doubt, the same cannot be said for Williamson. As the officer in charge of the boats it was his responsibility that the bodies of Captain Cook and the four marines were left lying on the rocks and not immediately recovered and brought back to the *Resolution*. While there was immediate difficulty in sorting out what had happened up to and during the affray, there was a fairly unanimous opinion that to leave the bodies for the Hawaiians to dispose of was a wicked and cowardly act. It was known to the crews that Hawaiians ritually cut up dead bodies, especially those of their enemies killed in combat; the ritual included scraping the bones of flesh and burning the flesh in a complex ceremony. The bones were generally kept and distributed among the important personages in the society. This was what happened to Captain Cook's body. The fact that Lieutenant Williamson did not play an active role during the affray, and in many people's opinion had actually sabotaged Cook's chances of survival by pulling further out from the shore, only made the failure to recover the bodies even more disgusting.

Samwell sharply and publicly criticised Williamson (Samwell, 1786). He said that Cook 'seems to have fallen a sacrifice merely for the want of being properly supported'. This was a view fairly common among the crews. According to Samwell, Phillips was so incensed at the lack of active support he and his men received from Williamson in the launch that he 'once thought of shooting him on the spot'. After reaching the pinnace and supposedly saving the marine, Phillips actually went back into the sea, this time to swim over to the launch, though we do not know what he said to Williamson.

According to Samwell (ms. Account), Williamson's men

spread a Report, that if they had gone in according to Capt Cook's Orders they might have given him & the rest of the people on shore some assistance, whereas in the Situation to which the officer had ordered them, they could be of no manner of service to any of the People; for all those who escaped with their Lives by swimming were taken in by the Pinnace, which was thereby so crowded that the Crew could not make use of their fire Arms against the Indians who were killing Captain Cook.

The desire of the launch's crew to get closer in was so strong that Williamson threatened to shoot anybody who did not obey his order to move away (Zimmerman, 1781). Harvey corroborates this in his ms. Log:

Had the Launch and small Cutter been as near the shore as the Pinnace it was a shame that they were not, it wou'd have gone a great way in saving some of those unfortunate men, for it was impossible that the Pinnace cou'd take them all off, in that confusion which was at that time without her being seizd and dragd on shore for one of them was seen in the water up to his chin very eagerly waving for the Launch to come to his assistance the launch's crew were eager to go to his assistance but the officer threatened to shoot the first man that pull'd a stroke; the whole action was so near the water's edge that the Captain & two others were kill'd in the water, supposing the Launch cou'd not have sav'd any of them, but by keeping closer in shore & kept up a constant fire, as they had plenty of ammunition, it wou'd have hindered the Indians carrying off the dead Bodys in that triumphing manner as they did beatg of them with Clubs whilest others were draging them over the rocks before our faces.

The difference that Williamson's launch would have made to the fire-power from the boats was in fact considerable. The three boats had about forty men in them, but during the action only a few were firing from the pinnace, and of those that fired most used only three or four cartridges.

There seems little doubt also that Williamson could have taken off the dead bodies (Bayly, ms. Log and Journal). After the shooting, Lanyon, in the small cutter, moved his boat from the point to the scene, and was ordered by Williamson to go in closer and fire at the Indians standing over the bodies. Accordingly, the small cutter with Lanyon and four midshipmen in it went in closer and started firing. By this time the *Resolution*'s big guns had fired a couple of rounds at the shore, which more or less cleared the rocks of Hawaiians. Mysteriously, the *Resolution* stopped firing as quickly as it began. Lieutenant Gore, presumably unable to see clearly what was going on, kept his shots to the bare minimum (Gore, ms. Log). If the *Resolution* had continued firing it would have been more than sufficient cover for a party to land from the boats and recover Captain Cook's body if not the others. But, even though the shore was clear, at no time did Williamson permit an attempt to be made to recover any bodies. His action in sending Lanyon in closer is therefore inexplicable. All he proved by this action was that his decision not to send a party ashore for the bodies was suspect. Samwell says (ms. Account):

They went in close but could hardly find an Indian to fire at, there being only a few Stragglers thinly scatter'd here & there, & the dead Bodies of Captn Cook and the four Marines lying on the rock close to the water's edge with only two or three Indians about them, so that there could be no manner of difficulty in taking them in. However one or two muskets having got wet in the Launch & abt as many men saying their Cartridges were almost expended, this was thought a sufficient excuse for returning to the Ship & leave the dead body of their great Commander exposed on the beach to the insults & Barbarities of the Indians. What can be said to this! – they did return on board with the Boats with about forty men in them, the major part of whom according to their own declaration, had their boxes nearly full, not having expended above 3 or four Cartridges; as they were pulling off, the Coxwain of the Pinnace fired at a few Indians on the Beach and killed one of them on which the rest immediately fled & left the Place clear.

The pinnace had pulled well away from the rocks after picking up the marine survivors. Williamson and Phillips were in the launch. The small cutter came off the shore, which was deserted except for bodies: about thirty Hawaiians were killed, and four marines, Corporal Thomas, Theophilus Hinks, John Allen and Thomas Fatchete, besides Captain Cook. Then all the boats pulled back to the ships. There were three badly wounded marines in the pinnace, one of whom, Jackson, the man Phillips had saved from drowning, was wounded in the eye (Trevenen; see Lloyd and Anderson, 1959). The Hawaiians had fled inland and were climbing the hill behind the village; silence descended on the scene.

The seamen, marines and survivors were stunned and exhausted with the excitement and tension of the previous twenty minutes. It was only now dawning on them that Captain Cook was dead. 'When they came along side they cryed out, with Tears in their Eyes that they had lost their Father' (Samwell, ms. Account). The dreadful news swept through the *Resolution*. 'Greif was visible in evry Countenance', and for the first half-hour the ship was almost totally silent as the news sank in. Some expressed their grief in tears, 'others by a kind of gloomy dejection more easy to be conceived then described' (Gilbert, ms. Journal). Lieutenant Gore sent Lieutenant Williamson over to the *Discovery* to give a full account of what had happened to Captain Clerke, who writes:

Lieutenant Williamson who commanded them upon this duty soon after came onboard the *Discovery* with the melancholy account that Captn Cook and four Marines had fallen in this confounded fray and that the rest of the marines who were onshore, were with difficulty sav'd, three of whom were much wounded, particularly the Lieut Mr Phillips who was a good deal bruiz'd by blows of stones and had receiv'd a deep stab with an Iron spike in his Shoulder.

According to Samwell, the Master's Mates, Roberts and Lanyon, made allegations to Lieutenant Phillips about Williamson's conduct and later Clerke held an enquiry: 'Several of the Boats' Crew were called who gave answers to the several questions that were put to them, agreeable to the Account that has been before given of this morning's transaction, but some of the Mates seemed to prevaricate and dissent from their first Assertions, even expressly contradicting what they had said to the officer of Marines when he blamed the Conduct of the Third Lieut' (Samwell's Account). The truth may have fallen a victim of rivalry between marines and seamen; the marines were blamed by the seamen for fleeing and the mates would not support the word of Phillips against one of their own officers. The result was inconclusive and Clerke did not proceed with charges against Williamson. Samwell (quoted in Kippis, 1788) notes that the depositions taken by Clerke regarding Williamson were not among his papers when the voyage returned to Britain. Clerke died of TB a year after Cook's death. Samwell speculates that Clerke might have decided that it was best to let the matter drop and that he may have destroyed his papers on the subject. It could just as easily have been the case that the papers were destroyed after Clerke's death by Williamson – he had motive and opportunity.

Feeling against Williamson continued to run high during the rest of the voyage. It is alleged that he fought a duel with Phillips at Cape Horn, but neither of them was hurt (Beaglehole, 1974, p.685). Home, the Master's Mate, accused Williamson of converting his boat crew to his side by making them drunk and persuading them to become masons (Home, 1838, p.305):

It was the intention of the whole of us to bring him to court martial upon our arrival in England but after Cook's death he came to be first Lieut. of the *Resolution*, and on our arrival at Kamschatka, he very knowingly established a mason's lodge, got all of the men to become full masons by bribing them with brandy, and got them to promise as brothers, they would say nothing of his cowardice when they came to England, so by this trick he saved his bacon.

It was not necessarily cowardice that caused Williamson to act as he did. In his surviving journals he showed a deep sense of grievance and he had clashed with Captain Cook on several occasions. At one time he said he would only do his duty if he could 'act from reason & the dictates of my own Conscience'. On this occasion reason and conscience may effectively have paralysed him. We know that Roberts was caught out by the sudden flare-up of violence, and Williamson was almost certainly just as much off his guard. But whereas Roberts' immediate reaction was to move his boat further in, Williamson's was to move his out. Gould (1935) writes:

I do not think he (Williamson) acted from cowardice on this occasion. It will be remembered that he had had to shoot a native at Nihau; and his journal of the events suggests he was no coward, but a good deal of a prig ... Of all normally good men, the high principled fanatic can, on occasion, be the cruellest – and such a man, I think, was Williamson. At all events, whether he was a fanatic or a coward, Cook's death must lie at his door.

One may or may not agree with this, but what is certain is that

Williamson got off far too lightly in the published account of the voyage by Lieutenant King. King completely ignored Williamson's part in the whole episode, and by doing this effectively silenced public criticism of his colleague.

Whatever accusations were being made, when Williamson stepped onto the *Discovery* with the news Clerke as the new commander first had to deal with the immediate situation. He went on board the *Resolution* and 'sent a strong party of People to protect the Astronomers at their Tents and Carpenters who were at work upon the Mast on the Eastern side of the Bay' (Clerke, ms. Journal). Bligh had returned to the *Resolution*, and Clerke ordered him to take the one manned and armed boat that was available (the *Resolution*'s cutter) and tell King the news, and also convey Clerke's orders.

King had been unaware of what was happening throughout the entire affray. According to his ms. Log and Proceedings, he was taking observations with the astronomers, and

did not see what was going forward in the bay, only that our boats were scattered about often in chase of Canoes, but in a short time the firing of Musketry at Kowroowa where the Captn was, so roused & agitated our Spirits that it was impossible to continue on observing. After some discharges of Musketry, & some great Guns from the *Resolution*, all firing ceased, except the *Discovery*'s letting fly two four Pounders at the People who were collect'd upon the wall ... no Gun could be better aim'd so as to miss doing execution. The first ball shot away a Coco nut tree in the middle, under which they were sitting, the next was as much too low and hit the rocks but in an exact line; as was natural this made the Indians move off.

The skill with which the shots were fired, which King mentions in his Log but not in his published version, is good evidence that Lieutenant Burney (who was left in charge of the *Discovery* while Clerke was absent on the *Resolution*) carried out precise orders to fire warning shots. From Captain Clerke's point of view, the action was appropriate. His attention had been drawn to the shore party, and Phillips could have reported the concern expressed by Captain Cook for the safety of the shore camp before the attack on himself. A glance through a telescope would show him a large body of Hawaiians sitting on and around the wall of the morai. The shots were the first defensive step to take before sending Bligh to reinforce the shore party.

King, however, wrote in his Log that he was 'exceedingly vexed' at the firing from the *Discovery*, especially as he had carried out his orders from Captain Cook and assured the Hawaiians near the observatories that they would not be molested. The majority of the people near his camp were women and children, as 'the Body of the people had gone over the hill to Kowrowa'. King decided that the *Discovery* had made a 'mistake', and to prevent them from firing again unless he wanted them to he sent his only boat to the *Discovery* with a request for a jack and pennant, which he intended to fly if he wanted the *Discovery* to fire to the right or left respectively. He told his· messenger to remind Captain Clerke that 'at present we were on the best terms & I had orders to keep so'. Samwell asserts in his ms. Account that it was King who requested the *Discovery* to fire the warning shots. He was on shore with King during this time.

King noted that 'we for about 10 minutes or a quarter of an hour were under the most torturing suspence and anxiety that can be conceived'. The firing had ceased, but it seemed to him he had been abandoned. His messenger had not returned, neither had his jolly-boat. The shore party had 'perceived some extraordinary bustle and agitation' at the spot where Cook had landed and 'afterwards saw the natives flying, the boats return from the shore, and passing and re-passing, in great stillness, between the ships'.

Bligh's boat pulled towards the shore, and even before he jumped out onto the black lava sand beach by the morai, Lieutenant King guessed what had happened:

I never before felt such agitation as on seeing at last our Cutter coming on shore, with Mr Bligh, he called out before he reachd the Shore, to strike the Observatorys as quick as possible, & before he announcd to us the Shocking news that Capt Cook was kill'd, we saw it in his & the Sailors looks. He could only tell us that he & some Marines were killd & their bodies in the possession of the Indians. Kiriekeea receivd this news as soon as we did, & asked if it was true, we thought fit at first to feign to disbelieve it, but to assure him of his safety, & advised him to tell Kao to get into a large house close to the Morai, which they did. (King, ms. Log and Proceedings)

Clerke's first orders were to strike the observatories but to continue the work of the carpenters on the mast. The mast was the key to the success· of the voyage for without it the *Resolution* was crippled. Clerke's observations from the ship on what was happening in the bay and his discussion with Lieutenant King soon altered his mind about the efficacy of keeping the work going on shore. The accounts that Clerke received from Lieutenants Williamson and Phillips rendered the Hawaiians, he thought, 'rather a formidable enemy'. The two shots from the *Discovery* had only dispersed the crowd behind the stone walls that abounded in the village. From these walls they could continually harrass. the shore party and the urgent work would be impeded. 'Had any unlucky accident gain'd them possession of the Fore Mast though only for a few Minutes, we should have been totally ruin'd in respect to another Northern Campaigne' (Clerke, ms. Journal).

King ordered his marines, and the men that Bligh brought with him, onto the morai. This gave them a good field of fire over the surrounding area, though it was less of a protection than it could have been since Cook had negotiated the removal of the wooden posts (a point King made in his ms. Log and Proceedings). The Hawaiians were seen all round putting on their war mats. The news of Cook's death had reached the people there by messenger from Kowrowa. The significance of this death was not lost on the Hawaiians; they knew it meant serious trouble. Once he had deployed his shore party with weapons on the morai, Lieutenant King took Bligh's boat to the *Discovery* (it being the nearest ship). He took with him the timekeeper, possibly the most precious item he had on shore. Without the timekeeper navigation would become a guessing game.[1] Clerke had returned to the *Discovery* to supervise reinforcement of the observatory party. While King was reporting to Clerke and receiving an account of his intentions regarding the carpenters the sound of musket fire at the camp was heard (King, ms. Log and Proceedings). The Hawaiians were attacking the morai party with showers of stones, and King could see 'several large bodies marching towards us, along the cliff' (King, 1784).

Bligh, who was in command of the party, had felt obliged to order his men to open fire. He had no intention of being over-run in the same manner as the marine party with Captain Cook. As the *Resolution*'s Master he had more than sufficient understanding of the necessity of protecting the foremast. King had given him orders to act on the defensive and naturally this did not preclude firing muskets if

---

[1] Hough (1972) suggests that this visit was to remonstrate with Clerke about the gun-fire; a careful reading of the ms. Log and Proceedings would correct this impression.

their position was threatened.[2] Fortunately the Hawaiians did not have very many Arees (warriors) among them at this stage and the fire had the effect of keeping intruders at a distance behind the stone walls and embankments.

King was despatched ashore again accompanied by reinforcements. All the boats of both ships were sent fully manned with armed marines and seamen. In all about sixty men were eventually deployed on the morai, which gives some idea of its size. Lieutenant Phillips had apparently recovered from his deep stab wound for he went ashore with some of his marines and took command of the action. The result of this show of force and selective firing at those Hawaiians who let their boldness overcome their discretion was that no serious attempt was made to attack the camp, although a large body of Hawaiians had arrived from Kowrowa. Clerke decided that the work of the carpenters would be best carried out without interruption on the ship and he issued fresh orders to withdraw everybody back to the ships.

By 11.30 everything and everybody was on the *Discovery* or *Resolution* (King, 1784). From these positions the visitors were completely safe as the Hawaiians would not try to attack the ships. Two schools of thought existed regarding how to react to Captain Cook's death. Neither school was identified by name, but the argument swayed between them for much of the next five hours, and intermittently over the next few days. One group of officers, probably supported by the bulk of the crews, was for a vigorous campaign of revenge against Hawaiians and their property; others, among whom almost certainly was Captain Clerke, were for reconciliation. King hints (King, 1784) that he was one of the party for forceful measures; Bligh in his marginal comments on King's volume states that King was 'one of the persons who were for l[enient] measures' (Gould, 1928b).

Captain Clerke decided to attempt to negotiate with the Hawaiians for the return of Captain Cook's body and for this purpose he sent Lieutenant King in a boat near to the shore, with a white flag, and instructions to make contact with whoever turned up to talk to him (King, 1784). It proved extremely difficult to secure Captain Cook's remains. King refused to accept invitations to go ashore and confessed

---

[2] Hough (1972) implies that Bligh was disobeying King's orders; but when King arrived back at the camp he participated in using force to dislodge 'some bold fellows who were attacking the shore party' (King, 1784).

he did not trust the people he was talking with. Other Hawaiians paraded just out of range making insolent gestures to the silently enraged seamen – some presented their buttocks in contempt – and a few could be seen wearing items of apparel from Captain Cook's body and those of the marines. Eventually, fragments of Cook's body were returned until they had collected what appeared to be the major part of his remains. These were deposited in the sea just outside the bay, in the traditional naval ceremony for a sea funeral. The rest of Cook's body remained dispersed over the island, and for many years after a small cult existed which worshipped the bones of Lono (Rev. Ellis, 1974, p.137).

Having completed the repairs to the mast, and engaged in some retribution against the Hawaiians, of which most were afterwards dutifully ashamed, they left Kealakekua, minus one of the ship's boats and Britain's foremost exploring seaman. It had been an expensive visit, though, given the choice, most present would gladly have sacrificed one of the two ships in exchange for Cook's life. It was too late. When the men he relied upon had had a chance to save him, they had failed miserably to match their actions to everybody's subsequent sentiments.

News of Captain Cook's death was sent to Britain overland across Russia when the ships called at Avacha Bay in May 1779. The message reached London some seven months later. The expedition continued with a northern voyage to the Bering Sea, and then a return voyage, touching at Japan, China, Africa and the Orkneys, to the Thames, arriving on 4 October 1780. Britain was then in the midst of war with the American colonies and the French, and attention was directed to the war rather than to exploration. The arrival of the *Resolution* and *Discovery* was something of an anti-climax, as the news of Cook's death was by then common knowledge, and the main achievement of the voyage – to prove that there was no practical passage from Europe to the Pacific by a northern route – did not require any action from the Admiralty.

Nothing that was said to the Admiralty by King or Gore implicated Lieutenant Williamson in charges of dereliction of duty. King and Gore were promoted to Post Captains, and the other appointments made during the voyage were confirmed. Phillips was promoted to Captain of Marines and Mrs Cook received a state pension in honour of her husband's work. From the official point of view the matter was closed; a tragedy, true, but one that all voyagers risked.

The task of preparing Captain Cook's Journals for publication and writing the official account of the Third Voyage was entrusted to Captain King, and when they appeared in 1784 the profits were distributed to the estates of Cook, King and Clerke (Beaglehole, 1974, p.685). Bligh received an eighth of the profits of the book (Munford, 1963a, p.ix). As was the custom at the time all journals, logs and narratives written by the men on the voyage were collected before the ships landed and were handed over to the Admiralty. (Several have since been lost; for instance Williamson's Journal is missing and so is Bligh's.) The Admiralty hoped to prevent unofficial publications from appearing before the official version and harming its sales potential; it regarded itself as entitled to a monopoly of the fruits of the voyages which it funded, and also to a first sight of any discoveries made. In this case the attempt failed – pirate books appeared as early as 1781 and continued to appear. Some may have been motivated by a wish to make a quick pound or two, but others were prompted by disagreement with what King published.

There is no doubt that King deliberately prevented Williamson's conduct becoming public knowledge, though why he did this is not known. Readers relying on King's version or the versions that copied him would have no idea of Williamson's part in the affair. King exaggerates the influence of what Lieutenant Rickman did at the southern point in Kealakekua Bay, and blames the 'fatal turn in the affair' on Rickman. If King told the Admiralty this and excluded criticism of Williamson, as seems likely from his published work, then this could explain why Rickman remained a Lieutenant for the rest of his career and Williamson was eventually promoted to Post Captain. That this was an injustice of the first order is now clear. Rickman obeyed Captain Cook's orders; Williamson failed to carry out Captain Cook's orders or to respond to the crisis. He did not use the means that he had at his disposal to save Captain Cook's life. But as King did not mention this circumstance he had to explain Cook's death by a tenuous train of events that began in another part of the bay altogether. Rickman was sacrificed and Williamson protected. Fourteen years later, at the battle of Camperdown, Williamson failed to attack the Dutch fleet with the vigour expected of a naval commander and he was afterwards court-martialled. He was found guilty of cowardice and dismissed from the service, though he put up a spirited defence and clearly thought he was unjustly treated (see Jackson, 1899). Some people who had been present at Kealakekua may have thought that justice had eventually caught up with him.

Williamson was not the only person protected by King. A careful reading of his book shows a hint of embarrassment at explaining Captain Cook's role. There is a suggestion that Captain Cook may have been too confident and acted a trifle rashly. But there is no overt criticism of Cook. The main thesis of the book is still that Cook was an innocent victim of an unexpected assault by people enraged at the death of the chief killed by Rickman. This can hardly be maintained if Cook's statement to King about making an example of Hawaiian delinquents and using ball shot to deter trouble-makers is considered. Cook's orders and actions made a confrontation inevitable. When he himself shot and killed a man in front of the crowd at Kowrowa, he did far more to ensure the attack on his person than Rickman a mile or so away.

Although books were published giving other views of the affair, King's version, by sheer weight of authority and numbers, formed opinions about Cook's death for nearly two hundred years. Samwell's writings opened up discussion of that part of the action suppressed by King, namely the conduct of Lieutenant Williamson. His writings were heavily drawn upon by the popular writer, Kippis, but Kippis did not mention Williamson by name, only by inference. William Bligh also criticised King's version. Bligh, as we have seen (p.82) laid the blame on the marine guard. Like Samwell he considered their conduct deplorable. They had fired in a panic and then fled as best they could leaving Captain Cook to the mercies of the mob. He went further than Samwell and blamed Phillips for having such a disorderly and undisciplined squad under his command. The evidence supports Bligh's remarks. If, as seems likely, he expressed these views to Phillips and King, it is no wonder that he was not promoted as quickly as he expected. If King was capable of suppressing Williamson's disgrace and of transferring the blame onto Rickman, he was not above a deliberate exclusion of Bligh's name from the record. Bligh accused him of purloining his drawings and charts and of failing to accord him credit for the navigation of the voyage after Cook's death. The fact that Bligh was paid one eighth of the profits of the published version strongly supports the contention that his work was appropriated and publicly attributed to Lieutenant Roberts – in effect, the Master was bought off to further the career of an officer.

From Bligh's letters we know that he was still angry in 1791 about what King had done to his reputation by crediting his work to others. He made his written remarks about his treatment in a copy of King's 1784 volume which was rediscovered in the Admiralty Library in 1928 (Gould, 1928b). Some authors have suggested that this was his own copy, taken by him in the *Bounty*, stolen by the mutineers and recovered from Pitcairn by the Navy many years later.[3] But it has been suggested by Lieutenant-Commander A.F.C. David, of the Hydrographic Department of the Ministry of Defence, that he wrote his remarks on a copy in the Hydrographic Office while he was working there in the early 1800s. Whichever it was, his charts and evidence which might have proved his point were lost with the *Bounty* mutineers, and his claims were never made public.

It is hoped that this small volume has contributed to putting the record straight. Captain Cook is deservedly revered in many countries for his contributions to human knowledge and the decency with which he went about his work. But that is no reason to protect his good name by doctoring the facts about his last hours and the actions of those involved in them. Nothing that Captain Cook did at Kealakekua could undo his reputation. After all, he paid the supreme price there for his mistakes. But what Lieutenant King did to the historical record, for whatever reason, has done real damage to the reputation of some of his colleagues and has given unjustified credit to the reputations of others.

[3] *Constable's Miscellany of Original and Selected Publications ...*, Vol. IV, *Adventures of British Seamen* (Edinburgh, 1827, p.322) points out that Captain Staines and Pipon obtained from Adams, the last surviving mutineer on Pitcairn, 'a copy of Captain Cook's first voyage which had belonged to Captain Bligh, and contained a number of marginal notes of his writing'; Owen Rutter (*Turbulent Journey*, London, 1936, p.118) notes that Bligh claimed compensation from the Admiralty for the loss of several books taken by the *Bounty* mutineers, among them a copy of Cook's *third* voyage.

Bibliography

Anon. 1779a. ms. *Account of the Events at Karakakoa Bay from 12th to 22nd February 1779, containing a detailed account of the death of Captain Cook and the recovery of his body.* Australian National Library MS 2427.

Anon. 1779b. *Extract from a pocket diary kept by one of the officers of HMS Resolution, 1779.* Archives of Hawaii, no. 3, Bernice P. Bishop Museum, Honolulu.

Anon. 1817. 'Real Cause of the Death of Captain Cook', *Naval Chronicle*, July-December, p.360.

Anon. 1873. 'Did Cook Knowingly Allow Himself to be Worshipped as Lono?', *Friend*, December, p.98.

Anon. 1907. 'Death of Captain Cook', *Geographical Journal*, December, pp. 668-9.

Anon. 1907. 'Description of the Death of Cook, by witness', *Sydney Morning Herald*, June 25.

Anon. 1926. 'Captain Cook's End as a Sailor Saw it', *New York Times*.

Anon. 1928. 'The Murderer of Captain Cook: his confession', *Pan-Pacific Union Bulletin*, June.

Ayres, James E. 1970. 'The Death of Captain Cook: Two Views', *Antiques*, May, pp. 724-7.

Barrow, John. 1835 (2nd ed.) *The Eventful History of the Mutiny and Piratical Seizure of H.M.S. Bounty: Its Cause and Consequences.* London.

Bayly, William. 1779. Ms. Log and Journal, PRO 55/20.

Bayly, William. (ed.) 1782. *The Original Astronomic Observations made in the course of a voyage to the Northern Pacific Ocean ...* London.

Beaglehole, John C. (ed) 1955-69. *The Journals of Captain James Cook on his Voyages of Discovery*, 3 vols in 4 (with portfolio). Cambridge.

Beaglehole, John C. 1967. *Captain Cook and Captain Bligh*. W.E. Collins Lecture, University of Wellington, N.Z.

Beaglehole, John C. 1974. *The Life of Captain James Cook*. London.

Bingham, Hiram. 1855 (3rd ed.) *A Residence of Twenty One Years in the Sandwich Islands or the Civil, Religious and Political History of those Islands, comprising a particular view of the missionary operation connected with the introduction and progress of Christianity and civilisation among the Hawaiian people.* New York.

Buck, Sir Peter H. 1945. 'Cook's Discovery of the Hawaiian Islands', *Report of the Director for 1944*, Bernice P. Bishop Museum Bulletin, Honolulu, pp. 26-44.

Burney, James. 1780. Ms Journal of Lt Burney with Captain James Cook 1776-80. British Museum, BM Add. Ms. 8955. (Also Mitchell Library, Sydney, Safe 1/64 and PRO 51/4528/45.)

Burney, James. 1819. *North-Eastern Voyages: A Chronological History of North-Eastern Voyages of Discovery; and of the early navigations of the Russians.* London.

Bushnell, O.A. 1971. *The Return of Lono. A Novel of Captain Cook's Last Voyage.* Honolulu.

Campbell, Gordon, Vice-Admiral. 1936. *Captain James Cook, R.N., F.R.S.* London.

Carruthers, Sir J.H. 1926-7. 'Captain Cook: His Last Days and Death', *Federal Capital Pioneer Magazine*, December (1926), pp. 14-20, January (1927), pp. 10-15.

Carruthers, Sir J.H. 1929. In *Sesquicentennial Celebration of Captain Cook's Discovery of Hawaii, 1778-1928*, Hawaii, pp. 44-7.

Charlton, W. 1779. Ms. Journals, 10 February 1776-26 July 1779. PRO Adm. 55/4557.

Clerke, Charles. 1779. Ms. Journal, 14 February-24 May 1779. PRO Adm. 51/4561. His ms. Account of Cook's Death is in the Mitchell Library, Brabourne Collection, A78-1.

Coffin, Joshua. 1875. 'Qbookiah on the Death of Captain Cook', *The Friend*, vol. 24, March, pp. 17-18.

Cook, James. 1779a. Ms. Journal. British Museum, Egerton Ms. 2177A.

Cook, James. 1779b. Ms. Order prohibiting unauthorised contact with Hawaiians. Dixson Library, Sydney. Ms. Q140.

Cook, James. 1784. See King, 1784.

Daws, Gavan. 1968a. 'Kealakekua Bay Re-Visited', *Journal of Pacific History*, vol. 13, pp. 21-3.

Daws, Gavan. 1968b. *Shoal of Time: A History of the Hawaiian Islands.* London.

Dibble, Sheldon. 1909. *A History of the Sandwich Islands*, Honolulu. (Originally published 1843.)

Dixson, W. 1924. 'Rare Pictures Relative to Australia (death of Captain Cook): notes of a Lantern Lecture,' *Royal Australian History Society Journal*, vol. 10, pp. 205-7.

Du Rietz, Rolf. 1962. 'Three Letters from James Burney to Sir Joseph Banks. A Contribution to the History of William Bligh's "A Voyage to the South Sea",' *Ethnos*, Ethnographical Museum of Sweden, Stockholm, pp. 115-25

Edgar, Thomas. 1779. Ms. Log. PRO Adm. 55/24.

Ellis, William. 1782. *An Authentic Narrative of a Voyage performed by Captain Cook and Captain Clerke in His Majesty's ships Resolution and Discovery ... including A faithfull Account of all their Discoveries and the unfortunate Death of Captain Cook.* 2 vols, London.

Ellis, Reverend William. 1825. *A Journal of a Tour Around Hawaii, the Largest of the Sandwich Islands.* Boston.

Ellis, Reverend William. 1974. *Polynesian Researches: Hawaii.* Tokyo. Originally published in London in 1842.

Ellis, M.H. 1964. 'The Killing of Captain Cook', *Bulletin*, vol. 86, February, p.10.

Furneaux, Rupert. 1960. *Tobias Furneaux: Circumnavigator*. London.

Gallagher, R.E. (ed.). 1964. *Byron's Journal of his Circumnavigation, 1764-1766*. Cambridge.

Gilbert, George. 1779. Ms. Journal. British Museum, BM Add. Ms. 38530.

Gilbert, George. 1926. *The Death of Captain James Cook*. Hawaiian Historical Society Reprints, no.5. Honolulu.

Gore, John. 1780. Ms. Log. PRO Adm. 55/120.

Gould, Rupert T. 1928a. 'Some Unpublished Accounts of Cook's Death', *Mariner's Mirror*, vol. xiv, no. 4, pp. 301-19.

Gould, Rupert T. 1928b. 'Bligh's Notes on Cook's Last Voyage', *Mariner's Mirror*, vol. xiv, no. 4, pp. 371-85.

Gould, Rupert T. [1935]. 1978 *Captain Cook*. London.

Hamilton, Sir R. Vesey, and Laughton, John Knox (eds). 1906. *Recollections of James Anthony Gardiner, Commander R.N., 1775-1814*. London.

Harvey, William. 1779. Ms. Log. PRO Adm. 55/110, 120.

Homes, Sir M. 1952. *Captain Cook R.N., F.R.S.: a Bibliographical Excursion*. London.

Home, Alexander. 1779. Ms. Journal of an Account of the Death of Captain Cook at Owyhee in the Sandwich Islands. Australian National Library (Copy in Mitchell Library, 923.9/H765/1A1).

Home, George. 1837. *Memoirs of an Aristocrat*. London.

Hough, Richard. 1972. *Captain Bligh and Mr Christian: the Men and the Mutiny*. London.

Howay, F.W. 1921. 'Authorship of Anonymous Account of Captain Cook's Last Voyage', *Washington Historical Quarterly*, vol. xii, January, p.51.

Jackson, Sir T. Sturges. 1899. *Logs of the Great Sea Fights, 1794-1804*. Navy Records Society, vol. XIV, London (in two volumes).

Kamakau, S.M. 1935. 'Kamakau's Account of Captain Cook', *Paradise of the Pacific*, vol. 47, no. 11, pp. 12-21.

Kennedy, Gavin. 1978. *Bligh*. London.

King, James. 1779. Ms. Log and Proceedings. PRO Adm. 55/116, 122. (Portion of same with variant readings is in the Dixson Library, Sydney.)

King, James. 1784. Third volume of *A Voyage to the Pacific Ocean; undertaken by Command of his Majesty, for making Discoveries in the Northern Hemisphere ... performed under the Direction of Captains Cook, Clerke, and Gore In his Majesty's Ships Resolution and Discovery ... In the Years 1776, 1777, 1778, 1779, and 1780 ... Vol. I and II written by Captain J. Cook F.R.S., vol. III by Captain J. King LL.D and F.R.S.* 3 vols, plus 1 vol. of maps and plates. London.

Kippis, Andrew. 1842. *A Narrative of the Voyages Round the World performed by Captain James Cook with an account of his life during the previous and intervening periods*. Originally published in 1788. London.

Kitson, Arthur. 1907. *Captain James Cook R.N., F.R.S., The Circumnavigator*. London.

Lanyon, William. 1779. Ms. Log. PRO Adm. 51/4558.

Law, John. (Attrib.). 1779. Ms. Journal of Captain Cook's Last Voyage. British Museum, BM Add. Ms. 37327.

Ledyard, John. 1783. *A Journal of Captain Cook's Last Voyage to the Pacific Ocean in the quest of a north west passage between Asia and America, faithfully narrated from an original manuscript by Mr J. Lendy*. Hartford, Connecticut. First published in London, 1781.

Lloyd, Christopher. 1949. *Voyages of Captain Cook*. London.

Lloyd, Christopher, and Anderson, R.C. (eds). 1959. *A Memoir of James Trevenen*, Navy Records Society, vol. CI, London. This is an edition of the C.V. Penrose ms. held at the National Maritime Museum, Greenwich.

Low, Charles R. 1876. *Captain Cook's Three Voyages Round the World*. London.

Maclean, Alistair. 1972. *Captain Cook*. London.

Mackaness, George. 1931. *The Life of Vice-Admiral William Bligh, R.N., F.R.S.* 2 vols. Sydney.

Manwaring, G.E. 1931. *My Friend The Admiral: The Life, Letters, And Journals of Rear-Admiral James Burney, F.R.S. The Companion of Captain Cook and Friend of Charles Lamb*. London.

Martin, John. 1779. Ms. Journal. PRO Adm. 51/4531, 55/123.

Munford, James K. 1963a. *John Ledyard's Journal of Cook's Last Voyage*. Oregon.

Munford, James K. 1963b. 'Did John Ledyard Witness Cook's Death?', *Pacific North West Quarterly*, vol. 54, no. 2, April, pp. 75-78.

New South Wales Public Library. 1928 and 1970. *Bibliography of Captain James Cook*. Sydney.

Payne, M. 1914. 'Admiral Burney and the Death of Captain Cook: some unpublished manuscripts', *Cornhill Magazine*, November.

Phillips, Stephen. 1926. 'The Death of Captain Cook', *Annual Report of the Hawaiian Historical Society*, vol. 35, pp. 64-8.

Pope, Dudley. 1963. *The Black Ship*. London.

Pope, Dudley. 1970. *The Great Gamble: Nelson at Copenhagen*. London.

Portlock, Nathaniel. 1779. Ms. Log. PRO Adm. 51/4531.

Portlock, Nathaniel. 1789. *A Voyage Round the World; but more particularly to the North West Coast of America: performed in 1785, 1786, 1787 and 1788, in The King George and Queen Charlotte, Captains Portlock and Dixon*. London.

Restarick, Henry B. 1972. 'Historic Kealakekua Bay', *Papers of the Hawaiian Historical Society*, no. 11, October.

Rickman, John. 1779. Ms. Log. PRO Adm. 51/4529.

Rickman, John. 1781. *The Journal of Captain Cook's Last Voyage to the Pacific Ocean on Discovery; performed in the years 1776, 1777, 1778, 1779*. London. Published anonymously and sometimes incorrectly ascribed to John Ledyard.

Riou, Edward. 1779. Ms. Log. PRO Adm. 51/4529.

Roberts, Henry. 1779. Ms. Log. Dixson Library, Sydney.

Samwell, David. 1779. Ms. Some Account of a Voyage to the South Seas in 1776-1777-1778, Written by David Samwell, Surgeon of the *Discovery*. British Museum, Egerton Ms. 2591.

Samwell, David. 1786. *A Narrative of the Death of Captain James Cook, to which are added some particulars concerning his life and character; also observations respecting the introduction of venereal disease into the Sandwich Islands.* London. Substantial quotes from this account appear in Kippis, 1842.

Searle, J.C. 1920. 'An Hawaiian View of Captain Cook's Death', *Hawaiian Almanac*, pp. 136-8.

Shankland, Peter. 1975. *Byron of the Wager.* London.

Sherton, J.T. 1937. 'Thomas Edgar', *Mariner's Mirror*, vol. 25, June, p.115.

Shuttleworth, W. 1779. Ms. Journals. PRO Adm. 51/4561.

Smith, D. Bonner. 1936. 'Some Remarks about the Mutiny of the Bounty', *Mariner's Mirror*, vol. 22, no. 2, April, pp. 300-19.

Sparks, J. 1828. *Memoirs of the Life and Travels of John Ledyard from his Journals and Correspondence.* London.

Stokes, J.F.G. 1930. *Origin of the Condemnation of Captain Cook in Hawaii.* London.

Taylor, W. 1779. Ms. Journals. PRO Adm. 51/4561.

Thurm, Thomas G. 1926. 'The Paehumu of Heiaus Non-Sacred', *Annual Report of the Hawaiian Historical Society*, Vol. 35, pp. 56-7.

Vancouver, George. 1798. *Voyage of Discovery to the North Pacific Ocean and Around the World ... performed in the years 1790, 1791, 1792, 1793 and 1794 ...* 3 vols. London.

Villiers, Alan. 1969. 'That Extraordinary Sea Genius, Captain James Cook', *Nutrition Today*, vol. 4, no. 3, Autumn.

Watts, John. 1779. Ms. Journal of Proceedings. PRO Adm. 51/4559.

Williamson, John. 1778. Ms. Log and Proceedings (fragments). PRO Adm. 55/117.

Wilson, W.F. 1926. 'The Place of Captain Cook's Death', *Annual Report of the Hawaiian Historical Society*, vol. 35, pp. 58-63.

Zimmerman, Heinrich. 1781. *Reise um die Welt mit Captain Cook.* Manheim. Translated as *Zimmerman's Account of the Third Voyage of Captain Cook*, by U. Tewsley, London, 1926, and as *Zimmerman's Captain Cook*, by F.W. Howay, Toronto, 1930.

Index

Allen, John, marine, 84
Atooi Island, 17 (*also named* Kauai Island, *q.v.*)

Banks, Sir Joseph, 10
Bayly, William, astronomer, 15, 43, 57
beer made from sugar cane, 21
Bingham, Hiram, missionary, 23
Bligh, William, 9; master of *Discovery*, 12; at Kealakekua Bay, 43, 52, 57; comments on Williamson's and Phillips' conduct, 81; sent to fetch King, 87; receives share of profits from King's account, 92; critical of King's account, 93
Bounty, 9, 94
Burney, James, 1st Lieut. in *Discovery*, 13, 29, 39, 46; his journal quoted, 52, 68; movements on final day, 56
Byron, Commodore, 11

Charlton, midshipman, 52
Clerke, Lieut. Charles, 8; in jail, 10; at Kealakekua Bay, 30; loss of cutter, 39; receives orders from Cook, 42; records events in journal, 45; movements on final day, 56; narrative of events at Cook's death, 73, 81; holds enquiry concerning Cook's death, 85; takes command, 87; tries to recover Cook's body, 90
Colville, Lord, 8
Cook, Capt. James, naval career, 8; relationship with Bligh, 9; with Williamson, 11; identified with Lono, 24; establishes friendly relations at Kealakekua Bay, 30; these relations undermined, 32; prepares to retaliate,

42; shore party named, 52; lands at Kowrowa, 53; activities of final day, 56; his death, 79; reactions to his death, 90

Discovery, 10
Dolphin, 10

Edgar, Master of *Discovery*, 12, 14; incident at Kealakekua Bay, 32; subject of report by King, 49; describes events at Cook's death, 74, 79
Ellis, William, Asst. Surgeon in *Discovery*, 15
Ellis, Rev. William, 69, 91

Fatchete, Thomas, 84
flogging in the Navy, 9
Furneaux, Capt., 13

Gardiner, James, 14
George III, 8
Gibson, Sgt., marine, 52, 65, 75
Gore, John, 1st Lieut. in *Resolution*, 11, 18, 45, 53, 56, 84; receives promotion, 91
Graves, Thomas, 8
Greenwich Hospital, 8
Griffiths, William, 21

Harvey, William, 67, 76, 78; describes Williamson's actions at Cook's death, 83
Hawaii, Cook's first visit, 7
Hermione, 9
Hinks, Theophilus, 84
Hollamby, William, 31

Home, Alexander, 15; journal quoted, 61; makes accusations about Williamson, 86
hostages taken as retaliation for theft, 50

Jackson, marine, 85

Kaikilanialiiopuna, wife of Lono, 23
Kaireekeea, priest, 25
Kakooa village, 23, 31, 35, 40, 51
Kamehameha, Hawaiian king, 24 (footnote), 31
Kanee-Kabareea, wife of Terreeoboo, 63
Kaoo, priest, 53, 88
Karakakooa Bay (*see* Kealakekua Bay)
Kareemoo, chief, 68, 70
Kauai Island, 27 (*also named* Atooi Island, *q.v.*)
Kawelo, warrior king, 27
Kealakekua Bay, 11; arrival of *Resolution* and *Discovery*, 22; return to, 28; description of shore, 40; departure from, 91
King, James, 2nd Lieut. in *Resolution*, 11; annoyed by Hawaiians, 31; involved in incident at Kealakekua, 33; appointed to investigate incident, 36; finds preparations to fight, 42; joins Cook in *Resolution*, 49; lands at Kakooa, 53; movements, 57; official version of final events, 67, 71; praises Phillips' conduct, 81; describes firing of *Discovery*'s guns, 87; receives promotion, 91; prepares Cook's Journals for publication, 92
Kireea, Hawaiian, 60
Kiverua, village, 60
Koa, priest, 25
Kowrowa village, 29, 38, 53

Lanyon, William, 42, 50, 52, 58, 76, 84
Law, John, Surgeon in *Discovery*, 79
Ledyard, John, 73; describes desecration of the morai, 26; refers to Cook's orders to Clerke, 46; account of events at Kowrowa, 59; relates incident of chief's death, 70; describes killing of a Hawaiian, 73
Lono, Hawaiian mythical figure, 17; legend of, 23; Cook identified as, 71

Matavai Bay, Tahiti, 10
morai at Kealakekua Bay, 15; significance, 24; description, 25; desecrated, 26; used for protection, 89
Mowee (Maui), 18, 28

Palliser, Sir Hugh, 8, 22
Parea, chief, 32; incident at Kealakekua, 33; complicity in theft, 38
Phillips, Molesworth, Lieut. of Marines, 12, 52, 56; describes Cook's visit to Kowrowa, 58; urges Cook to retire, 64; left on shore, 75; account of Cook's last moments, 77; conduct condemned by Bligh and praised by King, 81; promoted, 91
Pigot, Capt. Hugh, 9
Pitcairn Is., 94
Portlock, Nathaniel, 15

rations, as source of friction, 20
Resolution, 8, 10
Rickman, John, 2nd Lieut. in *Discovery*, 14, 43; under Clerke's orders, 46; on patrol, 57; fires on canoes, 68; blamed by King, 92
Riou, Edward, 15
Roberts, Lieut. Henry, 12; in command of pinnace, 42, 50, 52, 56, 75; makes allegations about Williamson's conduct, 85; Bligh's work attributed to him, 93

Samwell, David, Asst. Surgeon in *Resolution*, 15, 38, 65, 69; criticises Williamson, 83, 93
Sandwich, Lord, 13
Sandwich Islands, 18
sexual relations with Hawaiian women, 18, 31
Society Isles, 17

Tahiti, 10, 17
tapu (taboo), 29
terra australis, 8
Terreeoboo, Hawaiian king, 20, 25, 29, 40, 46, 60, 67
theft, by Tongans, 12; by Hawaiians, 30; of *Discovery*'s cutter, 38
Thomas, Cpl., 52, 84

Toe-yah-yah (Kawaihae), 28
Trevenen, James, 15, 52, 58

Vancouver, George, 15; involved in fight, 32; features in report by King, 49
venereal disease, 17
Venus, transit of, 8

Waimea Bay, 17

Wallis, Capt., visit to Tahiti, 10
Ward, midshipman, 52
Webber, John, 15
Williamson, John, 3rd Lieut. in *Resolution*, 11, 42, 47, 52; movements on final day, 56, 76; criticised, 81; protected by King, later courtmartialled, 92